Gift of
Mr. and Mrs. John Ruttle – 1965

CONCILIUM

THEOLOGY IN THE AGE OF RENEWAL

International Publishers of CONCILIUM

ENGLISH EDITION
Paulist Press
Glen Rock, N. J., U.S.A.

Burns & Oates Ltd.
25 Ashley Place
London, S.W.1

DUTCH EDITION
Uitgeverij Paul Brand, N.V.
Hilversum, Netherlands

FRENCH EDITION
Maison Mame
Tours/Paris, France

GERMAN EDITION
Verlagsanstalt Benziger & Co., A.G.
Einsiedeln, Switzerland

Matthias Grunewald-Verlag
Mainz, W. Germany

SPANISH EDITION
Ediciones Guadarrama
Madrid, Spain

PORTUGUESE EDITION
Livraria Morais Editora, Ltda.
Lisbon, Portugal

ITALIAN EDITION
Editrice Queriniana
Brescia, Italy

CONCILIUM

CONCILIUM/VOL. 5

MORAL THEOLOGY

MORAL PROBLEMS AND CHRISTIAN PERSONALISM

Volume 5

CONCILIUM
theology in the age of renewal

PAULIST PRESS
NEW YORK, N.Y. / GLEN ROCK, N.J.

Library of Congress Catalogue Card Number: 65-24045

Suggested Decimal Classification: 241

BOOK DESIGN: Claude Ponsot

Paulist Press assumes responsibility for the accuracy of
the English translations in this Volume.

PAULIST PRESS
EXECUTIVE OFFICES: 304 W. 58th Street, New York, N.Y. and
   21 Harristown Road, Glen Rock, N.J.
Executive Publisher: John A. Carr, C.S.P.
Executive Manager: Alvin A. Illig, C.S.P.
Asst. Executive Manager: Thomas E. Comber, C.S.P.

EDITORIAL OFFICES: 304 W. 58th Street, New York, N.Y.
Editor: Kevin A. Lynch, C.S.P.
Managing Editor: Urban P. Intondi

Printed and bound in the United States of America by
The Colonial Press, Inc. Clinton, Mass.

CONTENTS

PART III

DO-C: DOCUMENTATION CONCILIUM

PART IV

CHRONICLE OF THE LIVING CHURCH

PREFACE

Franz Böckle / *Bonn, W. Germany*

Coenraad A. J. van Ouwerkerk, C.SS.R. / *Wittem, Netherlands*

Within the general framework of CONCILIUM the moral section aims at giving guidance in the basic and practical problems of a genuine Christian moral theology. It is not so much concerned with purely theoretical explanations nor with normative solutions as with a clarification of the Christian's position in the present world. In the spirit of Vatican Council II we must think again about the religious and moral implications of our faith, so that we can proclaim it, as it is guaranteed by the magisterium, in a contemporary manner. In this way we can make Christian existence meaningful in a changed world. Many moral crises and uncertainties arise from a certain conflict that we experience between the demands of the Gospel and those of the world. The independence of the world, the basic inadequacy of man and world because of sin, the historicity implied in evolution and growth—all these factors have their consequences for Christian ethics, and this has not been given the attention it deserves. All this must be examined theologically and re-assessed as normative values.

The recognition of these facts requires a sound *theological* anthropology. And although this is primarily a matter of dogmatic theology, the dogmatic findings must be taken up and developed by moral theology. The real character of man's obligations and the assessment (essential and existential) of man's actions must be

1

derived from man's theological aspect as creature, subject of God's grace, sinner and redeemed in the light of salvation history.

We particularly want to explain what man is and what he must do in the light of this theological anthropology. Here we must begin by listening to what revelation tells us about man and by studying the basic structure of morality in the Bible (*e.g.*, its religious response, its christocentrism, its salvation history and its eschatology); we might then discover how much these structures correspond to the *a priori* and transcendental understanding that contemporary man has of himself. It should incorporate the findings of the positive sciences, such as sociology, biology, psychology and medicine. These findings, critically examined, must be embodied in the image of man, so that the Christian ethos will not be overlaid by secularization and relativism. Only in Christ can the world be saved in its totality.

The position of man in the cosmos also requires a careful examination of the relation between *man's personal situation* and *the reality of creation* as a whole. If we clearly understand the meaning of "creature", we must make a clear distinction between the immanent contents of human existence and man's essential, transcendental relation to God. Although these two cannot be separated, they do not mean the same thing but explain each other. This distinction might well be useful in reaching a better understanding of the disintegration caused in man and the world through sin, and the consequences of this fact on man's actions. God's incarnation confirmed the reality of the creation. It also shows that man is essentially related to God, which is important for salvation history because it implies that man must be integrated in salvation and must be delivered from the powers of evil. It is thought that the validity of a natural moral law in the order of salvation and the question of a religious practice which is turned toward the world must be discussed in the light of these principles.

The Christian man has a specific function in the Church as member of the Mystical Body and as citizen of God's People. Moral theology must take account of this *ecclesiological* existence, and the guidance it gives for Christian life must correspond to this.

This section must therefore show awareness of the various ways of life within the Church (marriage-celibacy, priesthood-laity, and the corresponding religious expressions of these conditions of life). It must also consider various personal vocations within the Church and their individual responsibilities. Catholic moral theology must be conscious of its responsibility for the whole Church without ever forgetting that "grace was given to each of us according to the measure of Christ's gift" (Eph. 4, 7).

A moral theology that takes its Catholic solidarity seriously knows that it is always responsible for the non-Christian world. This section would welcome an ecumenical dialogue with Christian denominations on basic and practical moral problems. New thought on the normative relevance of the structure of creation will remain vitally important. We must also examine again, in the spirit of the Council, the possibilities of cooperation with the Christian Churches in bringing about the evangelical formation of modern life in spite of differences in belief.

In the confusing wealth of opinion and endeavor the Editors will try to pursue a line which will meet all that is new in our time without losing contact with the great tradition of Christian wisdom. Only the whole of salvation history can show God's purpose with man. In moral theology they wish to treat objectively, honestly and critically of everything that happens in the Catholic Church in the field of morality. Open to all that concerns man and the world, this section will critically assess the moral views which are expressed in writing, conversation and not least in life itself. By trying to do this in a way that is scientifically unexceptionable we hope to make these views useful for those who are responsible for the care of souls.

PART I

ARTICLES

Coenraad A. J. van Ouwerkerk, C.SS.R. / *Wittem, Netherlands*

Gospel Morality and Human Compromise

not for refectory

If one has followed with some care the development of moral and pastoral theology during recent years, it is difficult to escape the impression that, behind all that has been said and written, there lurks a great deal of uncertainty where moral difficulties are concerned. Theology here reflects the doubt that besets pastoral care when, from one day to the next and all over the world, it has to face the discrepancy that exists between the Gospel and concrete life.

The problem of marriage today is a kind of junction where all sorts of questions and doubts of moral theology meet. But in other fields, too, such as politics and social life, it is difficult to know what to do about the conflict between norm and practice which we think we are experiencing. Clergy and laity reluctantly admit that various social factors and structures seem to force people of goodwill into situations which, by usual standards, are considered immoral. They cannot always cast off the feeling that in many cases these norms are a threat to the concrete requirements of life and lead to conflicts of conscience for which there seems to be no solution.

They have no wish to cast doubts on the possibility or actuality of sin, but they are no longer clear about where to look for real sin. Evidently, life pursues its own way with little regard for moral standards. In a complicated and widely varied world, life creates

7

demands that do not coincide in actual fact with what has been foreseen by our norms and laws. In spite of evidence and impressions, we want to take the Sermon on the Mount seriously, and the radicalism of the Gospel makes our doubt more acute and turns it into a problem of faith.

The question we hardly dare ask may be put briefly as follows: If we want to make sure that Christian life remains possible in this world, do man's imperfections and the disintegrated state of the world force us to accept a compromise? Or, can this amoral situation, the sinfulness of which can be doubted, not be justified *objectively*, even before God? Many are probably afraid to recognize their own doubts in this question. Yet, it becomes constantly more evident that a fair number of the clergy find it more and more difficult to be satisfied with subjective excuses that simply emasculate the above mentioned problem by appealing to constraint, faulty appreciation of values and other subjective factors.

No one doubts the significance and influence of these subjective factors. Modern anthropology and psychology have sharpened our understanding of them and have provided the plausible argument that in many aberrations there can be no question of a grave offense against God. One need only point to the difference between an important decision and a superficial choice, in other words, between an act *leviter moralis* and *graviter moralis*.[1]

Apart from the psychological limitations of our freedom, we have become aware of such factors as "moral impotence" which shows that even a calmly meditated choice can be subject to a pardonable inadequacy.[2] This appeal to the lack of a sense of responsibility on the basis of subjective limitations of freedom, is still adequate in many cases for a subsequent judgment, when we look in retrospect at the matter of guilt and sin. The fact remains that wrong has been done to someone else, and the next question

[1] Cf. P. Schoonenberg, *Het Geloof van ons doopsel* IV ('s Hertogenbosch, 1962), pp. 43–72.
[2] Cf. H. Boelaars, "Biechtpastoraal," in *Nederlandse Katholieke Stemmen* 58 (1962), pp. 218–29; *idem*, "Grondvragen omtrent onze pastoraal in verband met huwelijksmoeilijkheden," in *Jaarboek 1961 Werkgenootschap van kath. theol. in Nederland* (Hilversum, 1963), pp. 79–105.

is how to help the man who stumbled. The subsequent judgment remains free, since it is ultimately God who will judge; apart from this, such a judgment is inclined to be subjective and individualistic. The traditional morality of the confessional was accustomed to judge these inadequacies of man mostly in retrospect. Here it strikes us that this morality has hardly experienced the need to provide a theological justification for this anomaly in moral obligation.

It is significant that the conflicts of conscience inflicted on modern man cannot be solved exclusively by a retrospective judgment. One may expect that a realistic moral theology which is close to concrete life would give some indication of how to behave in the future. It must have the courage to look ahead. It cannot go on appealing to the lack of a sense of responsibility, constraint and moral impotence. Is it possible to justify, not only by subjective excuses but objectively, a situation that contradicts the general norms, at least at first sight? I believe that this question is valid and that we should not ignore it.

In fact, here and there attempts have been made to make moral compromise more objective. In connection with the problem of marriage there are constant references to the importance of broadening and developing morality. The question has been asked whether this process does not constitute an "objective" factor, a datum given in the concrete situation, and not merely a process taking place inside man. There is also a new emphasis on the fact that man is not merely bound to do the possible together with the demand that he must try to reach beyond the possible toward perfection; some wonder whether this provisional "possible" may not be put down to an *objective goodwill.*

In this connection we may point out that moral theologians are more and more convinced that the historical development of human ethics shows not only the influence of subjective factors (such as an increasing understanding of values), but also of situations (*e.g.,* the social and cultural form of a given society); some speak of a development of the norm itself.[3] Here, too, we see an attempt

[3] Cf. A. Wylleman, "L'élaboration des valeurs morales," in *Rev. Phil. de*

to give a more objective appreciation to a defective situation.

I do not pretend to provide decisive answers to all these questions. They are linked with various assumptions, opinions, interpretations and often prejudices that need to be analyzed more closely. I am more concerned here with the context and the unheeded implications connected with conflicts of conscience and moral needs. This leads inevitably to the questions of compromise and exception. My remarks are grouped around these problems. In this way I hope finally to show which paths lead to some solution for a concrete conflict of conscience, and which do not. This article must therefore deal with the boundaries of the norm for our judgment, and this might make some suspect that this is another attempt to excuse evil and to reduce the demands of the Gospel to a minimum. But I believe that if moral theology worries about the existential possibilities of Christian practice, it is genuinely trying to understand the will of God. Perhaps moral theology has been too glibly convinced in many cases that it could recognize this will of God.

HUMAN COMPROMISE

Traditional moral theology, too, has been aware of these existential difficulties: it offers certain ways of solving conflicts of conscience which, at least in appearance, look like a compromise. When we consider the Sermon on the Mount, there are certain theories such as those of the just war, self-defense, *cooperatio materialis* (material cooperation), which at first sight resemble a compromise. They give the impression of being negative and minimal, too close to a false kind of casuistry that has a bad name today. I want to concentrate on this apparent compromise for a moment as it might clarify the background and structure of a conflict of conscience.

The objections to casuistry, such as complicity or self-justifica-

---

Louvain (1950), pp. 239–46; E. Schillebeeckx, "De natuurwet in verband met de katholieke huwelijksopvatting," in *Jaarboek 1961* etc., pp. 5–61.

tion, spring up spontaneously and become stronger as we consider the arguments brought up in favor of it. They are not really convincing; they vary according to the author, and they seem to be the rationalizing afterthought of a conviction that is not clearly stated. This conviction is that the proposed solution *must* be right if life is to be tolerable and man is not to be forced to escape from it. The possibility to live a Christian life is accepted as normative although this starting point, apparently self-evident for many theologians, cannot be accepted as a principle. If, then, the possibility to live a Christian life forces us to accept a compromise, where do we draw the line? What we resent most in certain forms of casuistry is that it seems to sacrifice love to this "possibility to live" a Christian life.

Insofar as the cases mentioned above are concerned, many Reformed theologians see a real compromise: life in this evil world forces the Christian man to strike a bargain with love.[4] The Christian is forced to reckon with the structure of this world and to adjust himself to it, but nowhere in the Gospel can he find a justification for this deterioration in his moral behavior. This world, indeed, with which the faithful must reckon, and which is one of the elements that enter into his decision, is himself as a sinful man; it is his own work; it is the concrete realization of his own self. "The Sermon on the Mount does not overlook the reality of the world, but protests against it." [5]

The Christian can tolerate this conflict and this compromise in his faith, because he knows that God's mercy will not allow the "elements" of this world to deprive man of his love. For Protestant ethics there is no solution to this compromise, only a theological one. The Gospel condemns compromise *in any form* but saves man who must have recourse to it with a reluctance inspired by his faith.

In contrast to Reformed ethics, Catholic moral theology is based on the belief in the factual basic goodness of both man and world as being created by God, and this holds also for the situation after

[4] Cf. H. Thielicke, *Theologische Ethik* II, 1 (Tübingen, 1959), pp. 57–327.
[5] *Op. cit.*, p. 62.

the fall. Salvation can and must be realized through life within this world; salvation surpasses this world, but not in the sense that it abandons or rejects the structure of this world. To find out whether the emergency solutions in life can be justified before God, Catholic moral theology must again consider man's existence in this world. This reflection must, no doubt, be "in faith", yet it must consider life as "worldly". Moral realism and sanctity cannot be irreconcilable. It is therefore up to theology to develop a "worldly" understanding of the conflict of conscience and the emergency solution, because life in this world, which man tries to understand by reflection and experience, contains an expression of God's will.

Our faith also makes us ask whether the objection to compromise, that love is sacrificed to the "possibility to live", is really valid. When we analyze a compromise, the first fact that strikes us is that it is a matter of relationship and situation, not of conviction. Conflicts of conscience and emergency solutions impose themselves upon man as soon as his action involves him inextricably in a net of relations with human beings and things.

Compromise is often presented as if man, in his heart of hearts, prefers self-love to the love of his neighbor, and so capitulates to egotism and self-interest. When this is the case (and I do not exclude this factual possibility, of course), then there is no question of a compromise, but merely the choice of evil. The whole casuistry about love suffers from the fact that conflict of conscience is constantly presented as a conflict between two kinds of love; one then reaches the curious conclusion that egotism and love of neighbor live from one fall to another in a kind of psychological struggle for power in which they gain the upper hand alternately; sometimes one must love oneself more, next time one loves one's neighbor.[6] When love is seen as a conviction it knows of no compromise, nor does the world ever impose it as an inevitable necessity. The burden of conflict and compromise lies in the relationships, and affects the choice of various responsibilities with regard to the

---

[6] Cf. I. Aerthys and C. Damen, *Theologia moralis*, 17th ed. (Turin, 1956), p. 338.

world. Compromise forces a man to sacrifice one value to another though this value could be realized in a particular situation.

It is therefore unfair constantly to oppose compromise to heroism and a readiness for sacrifice. These relations are not formal and empty qualities of the situation, but indicate one's power and one's uselessness with regard to a particular issue. Heroism and readiness for sacrifice cannot decide what should be done; they only come on the scene when love has made it clear, here and now, what has to be done. He who sees in the words of the Gospel ("Greater love than this no one has, that one lay down his life for his friends") a clear condemnation of, *e.g.*, war, self-defense or separation of bed and board, evades the core of the question: What use is my self-sacrifice to others? and: What value gives meaning to my sacrifice?

The appeal to the radical demands of the Sermon on the Mount cannot decide whether compromise is acceptable in a Christian existence. The Gospel gives us parables of the kingdom, which suggest by way of illustration, what the kingdom of God can ask of a man who is impressed by this Sermon. It describes the possibilities of Christian sanctity that allows innumerable variations. This illustrative aspect of the Sermon singles out concrete situations in the context of actual life, and so explains the demands of radical love in a sharp and almost one-sided manner. It does not pretend to survey human life in connection with man's manifold responsibilities; nor does it attempt to include all the social consequences implied in the situation.

The Sermon does not tell us concretely how we should make our various obligations fit in with each other, nor does it deny that there may be many fellowmen who can claim our love all at once. What the Sermon certainly stresses is selfless love based on belief in God's love; but in many cases it is not clear what this love requires from us so that it can come into its own.[7] The Sermon shows the direction, but refers us back to the world to find there the way that will lead in this direction.

[7] Cf. R. Schnackenburg, *The Moral Teaching of the New Testament* (New York: Herder and Herder, 1965).

I do not wish to deny that the love revealed to us in Christ provides us with other criteria for the solution of various moral problems, including that of compromise, than, for instance, those of humanism pure and simple. Paul's Letters give several instances of Christian casuistry,[8] but Paul, too, knows of compromise as is obvious from the so-called "Pauline privilege" and from his acceptance of slavery.[9] Whoever, like Paul, is prepared to limit Christian freedom for the sake of mutual peace and the prevention of scandal, is bound to admit the necessity of compromise.[10] We cannot ignore the fact that the casuistic approach to war, self-defense, complicity and "white" lies, is definitely concerned with peace, mutual love and the vulnerability of the weak. Ultimately, however, Christian casuistry has to face the problem of what Christian sanctity means and how it can be realized. This leads us to the basic questions of grace, salvation and redemption in this transient era.

Modern moral theology has come to see that salvation and sanctity aim primarily at communion with the Father in Jesus Christ, and cannot be identified with a clear and unmistakable kind of moral perfection. Inasmuch as our communion with God is expressed in a just and devout life, it is realized *in mysterio*. We *believe* in a human and "worldly" order that contains salvation and holiness. The actual connection between our goodness in this world and salvation is not obvious and does not fall within the perspective of eschatological fulfillment.

The only criterion we possess of sanctity is love. In some cases salvation and damnation show through clearly enough in human situations and values; the permanence of sacramental marriage, the *porneia* (fornication) of 1 Corinthians 6, 12–20, and virginity stand out as moral relationships which appear with the clarity of faith as religious salvation or damnation in this world. In these

[8] Cf. Y. M.-J. Congar, "La casuïstique de saint Paul," in *Sacerdoce et Laïcat devant leurs tâches d'evangelisation et de civilisation* (Paris, 1962). pp. 65–89.

[9] Cf. 1 Cor. 7, 12–17; Philem. 61–62.

[10] Cf. 1 Cor. 8, 1–13; 10, 23–33.

cases the moral foundation and the motive of human action are surpassed and love of neighbor yields its place as norm to an immediately present religious reality. Here "God as all in all things" already appears within this world. Such an immediate eschatological breakthrough in life is hardly found anywhere else.

In general the form of sanctity must adapt itself to love of neighbor, and this love is tied to the inadequacy of man both in content and expression. Nowhere is love of neighbor linked with the promise of perfection whether of paradise or final fulfillment. On condition that it is humanly and morally justified, a moral compromise can be the best possible reaction of love, and as such it can be holy and "saving". All the newness of eschatological salvation, which we expect but do not know, makes it in any case impossible for us to use it as a criterion of perfection and total harmony for human activity.

One frequently has the impression that the enlightenment of the Spirit and the power of God's grace appear as a miraculous intervention in our world. In fact, all human life is borne on the nearness of God's grace in Christ, but God's grace does not compete with man and his potentialities and understanding. For the Christian, the structure of the world, character, intelligence and moral forces are not changed once and for all *in a divine way*. With the love poured into his heart, man must find his way in the world *in a human way*. The *gratia auxilians* is not a surplus of moral strength or moral insight that is added to human potentiality.

Our judgment of compromise, therefore, must not be influenced by some imagined picture of eschatological sanctity. We are once more confronted with the question: What does love ask of us? I have already mentioned above that compromise is not concerned with conviction and love but with a relationship. To many people this distinction between love as conviction and love as a relationship will appear as something unreal and dualistic. Moreover, in the Sermon on the Mount, Jesus does not merely demand a clear conviction but he also gives a decision on the deed.[11]

[11] Cf. Matt. 7, 21–27.

What remains of love if I kill a fellowman, abandon him in marriage or take his possessions, even if I do so reluctantly and in view of other values? There is no question about it; the Gospel demands love in action. Yet, I believe that there is again a danger of asking for an already realized eschatological perfection, under the inspiration of love. Love must be expressed in deeds, certainly; but can man realize this always, everywhere and in all circumstances? Love is a permanent requirement; but can it always express itself, show itself always and to all? Life itself forces us to maintain a distinction between love and deed; love implies a readiness and openness to do good, but these require a situation in order to express this in action. The one potentiality of love in man always faces many men and many tasks, but circumstances do not always bring these within its reach. In this sense we may certainly speak of a relativity of love.

When love cannot always realize its true intentions, we actively sacrifice values in most forms of compromise, which are vital for our fellowmen; we sacrifice his life, his bodily integrity, his honor, his security. With this we find ourselves at the heart of the problem of the inadequacy of man and the fallen condition of the world, of which compromise is a striking symptom. Man must choose, accept priorities, balance values and sacrifice them. In theory we cannot yet speak here of moral inadequacy, but rather of an anthropological one. Grace does not deliver us from this truly human inadequacy, although we often experience this as in contradiction with the final perfection we expect. The doctrine of original sin and of eschatological salvation gives theological significance to this inadequacy, and not only when this inadequacy leads to sin.

Yet, modern theology has taught us discretion in the interpretation of the *dona praeternaturalia* (preternatural gifts). How and in what way this fallen condition contradicts final salvation, and where redemption begins to restore it, we cannot say concretely. But if, perhaps, we have to accept the fact that compromise is the expression of an inadequacy in the eschatological sense, it does not yet mean that it must be rejected. Human existence forces us to choose and to make concessions. Where do we find the limit?

In the cases I have in mind the choice is always to the disadvantage of our fellowman: Is that to be accepted?

The conflict of conscience, for which we seek a solution through compromise, is often put forward as if it were a choice between a "moral" value and a vital "natural" value (one kills another in order to save one's own life). It is not difficult to see that this is an unjust way of presenting it. It is mostly a matter of two human values that cannot be reconciled and between which one has to choose in a moral situation (to take the life of another, to defend one's own). Nor is it a question of whether these values are relative in themselves, but the question is whether one can make them relative by looking at *one's own situation*.

It is evident that health, life, sexuality and so many other values are not identical with the absolute value of the human person. May a man make these values relative in his actions? This possibility clearly shows two limits: when the attack on someone else (with or without reference to a particular situation) is equivalent to a denial of his value as a person, it is morally unacceptable. Even in the case when one sacrifices a value that may be relative without motive and without counterbalancing it with an equivalent value, the compromise must be rejected.

After having stated these general principles, we must tackle the difficult problem of diversity. It is clear that Catholic tradition knows this relative limitation based on the human situation. Apart from the cases mentioned above I may point to two striking examples of this limitation of the absolute in morality: the Pauline privilege, which clearly limits the absolute application of the "natural" order, and the "safe period" which limits the meaning of procreation in sexual relationship. Isolated negative norms clearly indicate the rejection of certain forms of compromise, but then the difficult and uncertain task of moral assessment begins. The easy opposition of love and self-interest leaves us in the lurch; the various responsibilities and values must be examined and assessed. And here the final judgment ends with a choice.

Within the vast, fixed boundaries of absolute and negative norms there lies a wide region of moral uncertainty that we must enter courageously. Man will assess certain values in life differently according to the phase of development and culture in which he finds himself, and even within a given situation his judgment will vary according to the context. In the past, capital punishment and a just war were accepted in the Christian view; today they may have to be rejected in a changed world as unworthy of man. Particularly in emergency cases necessity can change the meaning of a situation in such a way that new values or new denials turn up and impose a new relationship.

I believe that Catholic moral theology has made room for compromise as described above. We have to speak of "compromise" here because we really sacrifice values which we give up only reluctantly and if it is necessary. Compromise does not attack love, but the harmony within our human existence is destroyed, and thus we shall always look on compromise as a manifestation of "not-being-redeemed" and we keep on expecting final salvation.

I have analyzed compromise against the background of the question of whether it is possible to justify an action which is at least outwardly immoral, and where the priest frequently doubts whether there is guilt. Can we speak here of an "objectively acceptable compromise"? In fact, in the conflicts of conscience I have in mind (in marriage, politics and social life) people will often speak of a conflict of values; hence there is at least an outward similarity with moral compromise as I have analyzed it in detail.

There is, however, a radical distinction between the two. The situation, which is generally considered to be objectively immoral and of which one doubts the culpability, obviously limits a value that cannot be sacrificed under any condition because it clearly contradicts a definite norm (e.g., it is said that the use of contraceptives limits in an unacceptable way the procreative aspect of intercourse in marriage). This objection seems to cut off any further investigation as meaningless and superfluous. But because of the questions and uncertainty connected with this problem, a closer analysis seems to me to be called for, if only to lay bare the heart of the problem. For the sake of clarity I want to analyze this problem in the concrete form of the use of contraceptives, although it occurs in other sectors of life just as much.

The Problem of Contraceptives

In this concrete conflict of conscience, too, the question is not essentially one of wrong conviction or disposition; nor is it essentially a matter of the inner acceptance of procreation as such. The problem lies in the situation, not in the conviction or disposition. It is therefore unrealistic to approach this problem as if it were a crisis of development: no doubt, a conviction can grow as it tries to express itself ever more adequately in the relationship. But in the case of actual distress in marriage this relationship itself has become a problem. The conflict lies precisely in that contraceptive intercourse is *no longer* experienced as a contradiction of love and of the function of marriage. The ethos of modern marriage rightly stresses the importance of sexuality for married life and the relative importance of the procreative function. This development has made the *situation* of contraceptive intercourse uncertain and difficult to understand.

I have pointed out already that love alone does not give a solution for the right interpretation of our responsibilities. Here this fact shows in an acute form. If the connection between our disposition (particularly where love is concerned) and our relationships were always clear and intelligible, there would be few conflicts of conscience and few moral uncertainties.

What modern marriage has highlighted is the fact that there is a conflict between the *experienced* and meaningful value of living together and the value of procreation which is not *per se* experienced. No partner will disclaim or deny that procreation has a meaning for married life, but he or she may find it difficult to put the normative value of procreation here and now in this concrete action on the same level as the felt significance of love. One cannot always say that in these cases there is lack of generosity and sense of responsibility where the begetting of children is concerned; if one talks of marriage difficulties, these lie in the fact that the sexual relationship, the *situation* of many people, has become uncertain and unclear. And that this lack of certainty about the procreative purpose of *every* act of intercourse is not a matter of mere fancy, can be seen from the fact that outside Catholicism moral philosophers and believers of serious mind and moral integrity have no moral objections to the use of contraceptives.

A number of married people no longer experience this conflict as a collision between two values, but as an opposition between a basic human value (love experienced in intercourse) and a *norm* which they themselves cannot see. If many have recourse to compromise, it is not for them a compromise between two human values, where procreation is sacrificed, but a compromise between a value which has meaning for them (love) and obedience to a norm which they receive from the Church. And so it becomes for them a compromise with faith.

We accept the fact that often in the history of moral theology different decisions were given on matters of life or possessions on the basis of the uncertain interpretation of definite values and their connection. In the case of the use of mechanical contraceptives the Church has ended this uncertainty by appealing to natural law. Since, however, belief in the Church is for many their only support in present-day marriage problems, moral theology will have to explain sooner or later on what the Church's *sensus fidei* is based when she rejects the use of mechanical contraceptives. The emphatic and intransigent rejection of contraception by the *magisterium* makes one suppose that the Church sees connections between this norm and *religious* reality, *i.e.*, the *salvation* aspect of marriage. But the moral uncertainty on this point grows day by day, and thus it becomes more and more difficult for Catholics to live by this norm.

Clearly, ethical compromise cannot answer the question whether in a given case an apparently immoral yet innocent relationship can be justified objectively. It would appear, however, that a curious situation has arisen here. As many experience a disparity between certainty in faith and uncertainty in morals, there develops a split, not to say a contradiction in their judgment, their sense of guilt and even in the norms they uphold. As believers they want to obey, but in their human moral experience they feel justified in deviating from the norm.

That is where the conflict lies for many, and it is on this point that they will compromise. Their situation thus gives us the impression that they are looking for moral justification of the situation. Here appears, perhaps, something of the discrepancy between salvation and life in the world, something of a theological inadequacy through which we believe but do not know what God's will was in the beginning. This inadequacy explains why one's situation may look justified from the human point of view but that one becomes conscious of moral failure through the faith. Modern theologians should look not so much for the justification of compromise as for the restoration of harmony between faith and moral awareness. That is the task for them today.

Jan H. Walgrave, O.P. / *Louvain, Belgium*

Is Morality
Static or Dynamic?

I

THE FREEDOM OF MORALITY

I would like to start this article[1] with a plea for the "freedom of morality". This expression is, of course, ambiguous and provocative. The grammarian will scratch his head and ask himself whether this genitive case, "of morality", is subjective or objective. Do I mean that I want to release man from the prison of morality that he experiences as an unwanted or unjust limitation of his freedom? Or do I mean to set morality itself free?

Freedom from Morality

At first, we might think, not without humor, of a deliverance from moral demands with a hymn in praise of man's spontaneous and instinctive strength. We might look for freedom in doing all those things which austere customs prevent us from doing; we might want to pull away the fig leaf, and to return to the state of *le bon sauvage*, man in the state of pure nature, unspoiled by civilization.

The "good man" in the state of nature is a myth that runs through the whole history of our civilization but that has lived particularly in the dreams of Western man since the 16th century.

[1] This article is based on a lecture given by the author to a congress of Catholic students in Groningen, 1964, the theme of which was "Freedom of Morality".

It reached its climax in the 18th century when the goddess of reason reigned supreme over the followers of the Enlightenment. There is an interesting paradox here. While in his mind man reveres reason and progress as the highest godlike values, in his dreams he cherishes the idea of a return to the good old state of nature and projects this dream into the myth of *le bon sauvage*— the good uncivilized man.[2] The pulling away of the fig leaf is equally ambiguous. Does this express the desire to return to the prehistoric innocence of Adam and Eve at the dawn of creation, when they still did right unconsciously, without law or compulsion? Or does it express the desire to allow full play to one's instinct without bothering about law or sin? Is the idea to break with the morality of a corrupt civilization in order to return with Rousseau to the goodness of pure nature? Or is it to rise with Nietzsche above good and evil toward a type of man who will no longer know the hesitations and torments of conscience?

These are two old dreams. Ovid wrote nostalgically about the *aurea aetas* (the golden age), which the Greeks dreamed of before him, and in which man did no wrong *sponte sua sine lege* (spontaneously and without laws). Is not Prometheus the eternal symbol of man despising the will of the gods in order to control his own destiny in freedom and the exercise of his own power?

Is the choice, then, between a romantic breakthrough, downward, to a natural innocence, and a demonic breakthrough, upward, to a deliberate denial of guilt? Or is there a third choice, that of authentic Christianity, which made St. Thomas say that the New Law is the law of perfect freedom? It is called the law of perfect freedom because Christ demands nothing else than what is necessary for salvation in terms of morality and love, and because he gives us his Spirit through whom love rises in us, spontaneously alive.

Freedom of Morality

And so we reach the second view of our theme: not freedom *from* morality but freedom *of* morality. It could be described as

[2] See H. Baudet, *Het paradijs op aarde* (Assen, 1959).

"he who makes morality free, frees himself" or "authentic morality". This means that the basis of our life ought to be, not the
compulsion of a universally accepted morality, but the release
brought about by a personalist morality.

Morality itself must be freed, therefore. First of all, it must be
freed from "the compulsion of what is universally accepted, and
therefore taken as valid"; in other words, from a conception by
which morality is experienced as oppressive, not because it is universally valid—the law of love is no less universally valid—but
because the way in which our society accepts it universally is no
longer authentic, no longer corresponds to the personal convictions
of our personal conscience.

This takes us straight to the heart of our problem. It should be
pointed out at once that the ambiguity mentioned above may well
turn into a meaningful paradox. Perhaps "to free morality" is the
same as "to free ourselves from morality". When we release morality from the social compulsions which turned morality into a
matter of habits and customs in order to make it spring up again
within ourselves as its true source, we free ourselves indeed from
the compulsion of morality. We thus regain our freedom, not in
immorality, but in authentic morality.

Much contemporary thought centers on this theme. The contemporary crisis in morality is the deepest expression of the historic crisis in human existence within which we move. The protest
against the unauthentic morality of the *plebs* (the common people),
as Kierkegaard called it, or of "they" (in German: "man"), as
Heidegger put it, or of "the others" (*les autres*), in the terms of
Jean-Paul Sartre, is but the negative aspect of this crisis. Contemporary man wants to be free from that. But what is the positive
purpose? Here the roads diverge. Is all morality only a morality
of "the others"? Should we deny that there is anything objective
and normative in morality, and make our freedom the one and
only decisive factor of the moral values we wish to accept? Are
we alone the creators of the purpose of our existence? Is there no
norm that can bind us except the one we ourselves accept as
binding?

Some existentialist thinkers answer this question bluntly in the affirmative. But there are those who, with Kierkegaard, Newman and others, unmask the spurious objectivity of social morality in order to recall man to the true objectivity of the authentic conscience. This spurious objectivity derives from a process by which historical patterns of behavior have become social conventions in the collective awareness of a society, and are thus taken as the expression of our unchanging nature. True objectivity is lived evidence; it invites us to respond with generosity and love, and this response springs from the consciousness of our freedom that is the basis of our humanity.

We should outline as carefully as possible the differences and agreements in the progressive dynamic tendencies that emerge from contemporary morality. All agree on the *terminus a quo*, the starting-point, namely, the moral behavior that they reject. They do not agree on the *terminus ad quem*, the end in view, namely, the kind of moral conduct that they wish to bring about.

The *terminus a quo* of these tendencies is a morality, a form or style of moral behavior, that is experienced as untrue or unauthentic for two reasons.

First, the concrete norms of this behavior no longer correspond to the moral awareness of our generation in various ways. Second, the appeal of these norms remains extrinsic to us: we carry them around in us, but we do not experience or accept them as inspired by our own personal conscience. They are the social tenets of the environment that has shaped us, has conditioned us historically and influences our behavior mainly by unconscious social pressure. For these two reasons this morality is rejected as untrue, foreign to our personality: it is historically out of date and it affects us through social pressure.

But there is a connection between these two reasons. This social morality, rooted in an unquestioned absolutization of historical patterns of behavior, denies its own historicity and is therefore essentially static and conservative. In an age that is marked by a rapid development of man's historical situation, the difference between this morality and the moral experience of life grows wider and wider, and its claim on individuals weaker and weaker. Man experiences an increasing tension between the established norms, embodied in the social condition of his personality, and the new norms which the historical situation seems to impose. He experiences this current morality—easily identified with morality as such —as a burden and an alienating force.

The main issue in the present debate is the *terminus ad quem*. We want a morality in which we can behave as persons, that we freely accept as persons, and that suits the historical situation in which we live. But what can we take as our basis? How can we answer for the moral course we want to adopt?

Should we simply ask ourselves: "What do I really want?" and then arrange our behavior accordingly, without bothering further about responsibility? Should we take it that our freedom itself is the sole source of the norms of our conduct and moral values, and then accept the fact that this freedom is absurd, *i.e.*, has no responsibility beyond its own decision: "I want it like this because I want it like this"?

Or should we follow the English positivist humanists and reduce moral problems to purely technical ones? Life has to be ordered if we want to avoid chaos. Should we, like Coates in his humanist manifesto,[3] maintain that there is not really much difference between moral problems and the management problems of a tennis club; that the only thing that matters in any situation is to reach a conclusion that best serves the interests of all involved?

Or should we base ourselves on the highest ethical norm that we recognize as objective, intangible and not subject to any personal whim in the very roots of our conscience and moral awareness? This is the position of the Netherlands Society of Humanists,[4] and also that of Christian personalism.

[3] J. B. Coates, *A Challenge to Christianity* (London, 1958).
[4] "Humanistisch Verbond" is a Dutch organization, founded in 1946, to provide a focus and center for all people who wish to interpret and build up the world on the spiritual and moral power of man alone, without the assumption of a personal God and a special revelation. The keynote is respect for the human person, his freedom and responsibilities within the community. It is this organization which took the initiative in founding the International Humanist and Ethical Union (I.H.E.U.) in 1952.

II

DEVELOPMENT AND TRUTH

It is not my purpose here to attempt to solve the general problem of contemporary morality. I would rather limit myself to a preliminary question, of the utmost importance for every individual case, namely, can there be a development in morality? What does it mean? How can it be justified? In order to understand this point we must proceed with order and clarity.

1. The first point to be clarified is to know what we are talking about. What is morality? The word is used in various ways although they all have something in common. In the first place, morality means the norm or complex of norms that man thinks must guide him in his freedom. Morality, therefore, belongs to what constitutes the human phenomenon, *le phénomène humain*. It presupposes freedom, without which there can be no morality. A free being has a choice of actions, and since man is a being in which freedom is embodied and "situated", the choice of his freedom will be influenced in many ways by the biological interplay of instincts and emotions. Because he is free he can choose; because his freedom is embodied in the flesh he is pulled in many directions. Morality begins at the point where a man says to himself: "Although I can do this or that and feel inclined to do this rather than that, I do not want to be pushed by whims or fickle emotions. I will let myself be guided by certain fixed rules which I feel myself bound by, or which I want to impose upon myself."

I have kept the description of this human phenomenon as general and neutral as possible. Morality can then mean either the norm which man imposes upon himself, or the science of that norm (the study that analyzes and tries to justify the concept of this norm: ethics), or living according to these norms (moral conduct). Our study is mainly concerned with the first meaning of morality, the norm freely imposed upon oneself and the connected problems, such as its basis, validity, and so on.

In morality we also distinguish between moral science and moral conduct. The science studies the norm as norm; moral conduct is rather a sociological concept and the norm is studied by sociology as a fact. Every human community in fact follows certain patterns of moral behavior that are bound up with the total pattern of a given culture. Morality is then the sum total and pattern of the moral behavior and customs that obtain in a given society. Various Christian countries, for instance, show different kinds of morality which partly conform to, and partly diverge from, the precepts of Christian morality. The sociologist will try to explain this by referring to the historical growth of the overall cultural pattern of a given region.

2. Morality, then, is the norm or the totality of the norms to which freedom is subjected. Where do we find that norm? Not, of course, in material things. It lives in man's consciousness, in his thought. Whatever the basis of the moral norm, it is essentially a "thought".

Hence our second question: Can there be a development in this morality, *i.e.*, in man's thought about these norms, their foundation and validity? That there is a certain development is an irrefutable fact, but is this fact intelligible?

Here we are helped by one of the most important insights of contemporary philosophy that not only makes development comprehensible but also provides a certain ground for justification. This is the insight into the essential historicity of human existence to which human development is essentially linked.

Historicity does not simply mean that man *has* a history, just as he has clothes or possessions, but that he *is* history, just as he is flesh and blood. The classical definition that man is a rational being could well be replaced by such definitions as "man is a cultural being" or "man is an historical being", which are equally valid. That man is an "animal" means that he is bodily present in this world; that he is also rational means that his existence in the world is a conscious existence, *i.e.*, an existence that thinks about itself, interprets itself and its world through this thinking, and builds up its life and its world on the basis of this thinking. An existence that unfolds itself creatively through thought in the material world is precisely what we mean by an historical existence.

The proper character of man, his "humanity", is not a natural product predetermined in the human organism by birth. Man's humanity is given only as a pure potentiality which must be realized by his own thought, freedom and responsibility. Human existence is therefore not so much a datum as a task and a vocation. The results of this life which realizes itself through thought constitute culture. The dramatic epic of creative human existence constitutes history, which, therefore, is the peculiar existence of a free and thinking being in a material world. History is the perpetually moving result of the constant interplay between man, who in conscious freedom tries to realize himself, and the changing historical situation composed of many objective factors that confront this freedom.

The situation is the sum total of all the factors inherent in our existence, factors that are not freedom but confront it. On the one hand, they spring from nature of which our body with its inherited bio-psychological qualities is a fragment; on the other, they are produced by our creative freedom that changes nature constantly and introduces new factors into the objective world. These objective factors that freedom leaves behind in nature constitute objective culture. Nature, constantly modified by objective culture, constitutes the changing situation that confronts human freedom from generation to generation in ever varying ways. The dialogue between man's conscious freedom and the objective factors of our situation constitutes history.

Man is a history; he is, as Ortega y Gasset says, a narrative, a drama of which he himself is both author and leading actor. The development of this narrative is partly predictable, insofar as the objective factors determine from one moment to the next what is possible or urgent and so make man undertake concrete tasks commanded, so to speak, by the situation. Partly, however, it is unpredictable, insofar as conscious freedom can choose between various possibilities and interpret the situation in various ways, rightly or wrongly. Man is the only animal that can fail because his reaction to the circumstances of life is not infallibly determined by natural instinct but by the fallible activity of conscious freedom.

The basic factor of history is, therefore, conscious thought,[5] the free and creative interpretation of the situation and the answer to it. This conscious thinking introduces freedom into the situation and brings the situation within the scope of freedom. Our life, indeed, is not influenced by circumstances as they exist by themselves outside us, but as they are interpreted by human thought. Thought turns brute circumstance into human situation, and makes this a human world.

On the other hand, thought also introduces the situation into our freedom. It is proper to "embodied" and "situated" freedom to interpret the world creatively and change it, and so change its own situation in the world. Man is an animal that constantly transforms his being and his environment, *i.e.*, the nature and society that surround him, through his thought and action. In this way he changes the conditions of his existence, his life, and ultimately himself. But this presupposes that he cannot rest content either with himself or with his condition as determined by the nature and society in which he lives. This is, however, only possible through a creative imagination that can see things, not as they are, but as they could and should be.

The quality of a thinking existence that sees the world and itself not merely as a fact, but also as a potentiality and a task, consti-

---

[5] The terms "thinking", "thinking existence" and "thought" are not used here in a purely intellectual sense. To think is not the operation of an intelligence which is enthroned above life and separated from it. It is the active, reasoning and progressive aspect of our whole conscious life; it is not an inoperative contemplation, but a constant pondering upon and restless striving after clarity. To think, therefore, is our whole consciousness, active and alive. Love, for instance, is not the same as thought, and yet it is "thinking" in a certain way. Love can live only in the constantly progressive discovery of "the other" person as an objective value. But this discovery through thought involves the whole person, and is not a matter of an *intellectus separatus*, a reason which stands apart from the rest of the person. Man moves as a whole, Newman said. Whether he will discover in the other the precious hidden pearl of an exciting personal value does not depend on his intellectual power but on the basic moral attitude which manifests his personality. Love, as a basic attitude, conditions the thought that will see in "the other" an invitation to love.

tutes human existence. It allows man to project an imaginary world which does not exist but which he can actually turn into reality. This free and thinking existence creates culture because it aims at a self-realization and a corresponding world-realization that man himself projects. Insofar as this task inspires and moves man because it seems good and desirable to him, it is called "value". Insofar as it is not yet realized but exists only in the mind, it is called "ideal". Culture is the realization of values or ideals in nature.

It is, however, obvious that man is not led by abstract and general values and ideals. The true, the good, the beautiful and the noble are, no doubt, absolute values. But they do not move us as pure ideals; they move us insofar as they are expressed in concrete tasks. The possible, the here and now attainable, the concrete invitation, are determined by the situation in which man finds himself.

In our life our freedom is no more determined by absolute idealism than our situation is determined by brute circumstance. It is thought that turns the absolute ideal into a concrete inspiration, just as it turns brute circumstance into a human situation. It transforms opaque facts into situations illumined by ideal values; it transforms the pure light of the ideal into embodied values made concrete in the situation. The ideal interpretation of circumstance and the situational interpretation of the ideal form an indivisible unity, the typical unity of man as a thinking or historical being.

This thinking or historical existence, through which man constantly transforms his world and his life, is nothing but the process of human self-realization. Human existence or humanity is a task, of which history is the realization. It is man *in fieri*, man in the process of constant growth and development.

We could sum all this up in a brief argument: if humanity is essentially a task, and therefore a becoming, then historicity is evidently an essential dimension of humanity. Human existence is history. And if thinking is the fundamental activity of man's becoming, then historicity is above all a quality of this very thinking.

From here we can go on without difficulty: if morality is a product of human thought, then morality, too, is essentially historical and constantly involved in development. Morality is the totality of the norms, imposed on our thought by the ideal. This ideal is expressed in concrete terms according to the demands and possibilities of the constantly changing and developing situation.

3. Morality, then, like everything human, is marked by essential historicity. Can we form some idea of the dynamism that keeps this historical development going?

A general idea, at least, is possible. The dynamism of man's moral development is dialectic, an interplay of two opposed tendencies. On the one hand, morality shows an inclination to become "established", fixed in moral conduct, in patterns of social behavior, set up to satisfy the needs of the community and sanctioned by social pressure.

On the other hand, the human person who values his authenticity will try constantly to break through a moral code that threatens his integrity and to restore genuine morality in life. This is the counter-tendency that tries to set morality free from a moral code and to deliver man from the coercion of fixed customs in order to lead him back to authentic morality.

When we survey the history of morality we can see that this interplay of morality and moral codes moves, through various fluctuations, in the direction of a constantly clearer and firmer assertion of a personalist morality over against a group morality. Primitive man is wholly imprisoned in the group morality. Contemporary man demands a personalist morality more universally and more intensely than ever. We see here, therefore, a dialectic process, a struggle between two tendencies, the result of which seems to show a more and more pronounced triumph of personalist morality, or, in dialectical terms, a synthesis in which code morality is ousted by true morality. This means that the ideal phase toward which history is progressing is that in which true morality will completely transform the morality of the community.

But this progress is not inevitable. We can always slide back. Not only should we foresee periods of relative decline, but the struggle will probably never cease in the history of mankind. The

tendency to slip into a fixed and degrading code morality is inherent in our historical existence. That is why, with all our radical
straining after an authentic morality, we should be wise enough to
recognize that some code morality is relatively inevitable, although
we should at the same time fight these tendencies intelligently.
The *growth* of humanity is the sense of history and in this world
it will never attain its goal absolutely and completely. We must
constantly strive after what is best even when only the better is
possible.

4. We must still confront here the contemporary recognition of
historicity as the basic feature of human thought, with the basic
feature of the truth which is the object of this thought. Is the truth
not by nature absolute? What is true is true without more ado.
Does this not conflict with the essential historicity of thought?
Does historicity not imply that what counts as true is determined
by the historical situation and so differs, according to time and
place? As Pascal said mockingly: "How agreeable it is to determine justice by a river boundary. Truth is on this side of the
Pyrenees, error on the other side." And what we see today as true
and good, we reject tomorrow as untrue and improper.

The answer to this question lies in our basic argument. History
is the growing process of humanity in an uninterrupted attempt
at self-realization through thought trained upon truth. This means
that history, as an aspect of our thought implies the growth of
truth in our thinking existence. In everything we begin with nothing. Freedom is not something that is given, but something that
is acquired. This holds also for the truth in our thought. The
growth of our humanity is in a sense the growth of truth in our
thought.

One of the basic insights of contemporary philosophy is that we
live in a pre-reflective consciousness of the truth. In a certain sense
we exist in the truth before we think it explicitly. According to
Heidegger, the characteristic way in which man exists is marked
by the fact that, before reflection takes place, man is already aware
of the mystery of the reality in which he lives and of which he is a
part. Thought, both as a spontaneous experience and as reflection,

is an attempt to bring this mystery to the light of full consciousness by means of concepts and words. This clarification is truth in the proper sense. Truth is reality as no longer secret, says Heidegger. Thought, therefore, is the attempt to unveil that mystery of reality, to take it out of the secrecy of pre-reflective awareness into the openness of explicit knowledge. History is the process of our self-realization through a constant unveiling of the truth.

Thought, therefore, takes place within a pre-reflective awareness of the truth. But it is not a simple and straightforward unveiling. It is an interpretation by means of ideas which well up in us or which we form ourselves. We clarify the world of our experience by means of ideas which are the product of our thought; the world we experience becomes the object of our explicit consciousness only in and through those ideas. Our whole life plays a part in this production of ideas, this interpretation: all the factors of our historical and individual situation, our dispositions and inclinations, the traces left in our personality by education and destiny, all this contributes to it.

This means that this interpreting reflection, however guided and prompted by a pre-reflective and unconsidered awareness of the truth, remains essentially human: it starts from a limited perspective, is functionally bound up with the problems of our age and of our personal life, subject to all the influences of dispositions and inclinations, hampered by the blinding arrogance of our sinful existence but also helped by the grace of God who opens our heart to the truth in humility.

All these factors together make up that complex historical process, full of tensions and oppositions, conflict and bias, changing emphasis, one-sidedness, generalizations and errors.

Yet, in the midst of this wild adventure there is unmistakable progress, a laborious pushing on in the direction of the truth. The present, indeed, carries the past in itself as an essential aspect of its actuality. The lessons of the past become richer and clearer all the time. Ideas of all kinds are put through the mill of historical experience and are eliminated as useless errors. Every age has its errors and its values but the total process creates nevertheless a constantly expanding synthesis of the truth. Thus man's historical search for himself is also a search for the truth. However, we get no glimpse of an absolute and final achievement. The approach to the truth becomes richer and clearer. But, as Merleau-Ponty says, "There is no thought which embraces all our thought".[6]

No product of reflection can ever coincide with the fullness of the truth in which we exist in a pre-reflective way, but reflection is inserted in this pre-reflective thought. Awareness of the truth is the transparent background for the laborious efforts of our thought. Through our ideas, our concepts and symbols, the careful handling of our words, we reach out to the invisible presence of the truth in us; we aim at it, we approach it. In this way we reach the truth itself, however inadequately, or rather we *can* reach it, we can approach it, we can purify our thinking of more and more errors. The truth lives in us as something open, a disposition for more truth, for correction and completion.

This can be summed up in a few words. Although the truth is absolute, our knowledge of the truth, our vision of it, remains human, limited, inadequate, perfectible, straining between a pre-reflective, unillumined awareness of the truth and the laborious, changing historical efforts of our thought to absorb this truth in our conscious life. In the end, the historicity of our thinking simply means that our knowledge of the truth is human and imperfect, and will remain so as long as we are on earth.

III

TOWARD AN AUTHENTIC PERSONALIST MORALITY

The whole argument so far may have made it clear that the historicity of morality does not mean relativism and that we are on the way to a *personalist* morality through a complex and not necessarily effective process.

The source of authentic morality is the conscience, *i.e.*, our conscious and free acceptance of a call to generosity and unselfishness.

[6] M. Merleau-Ponty, *Phenomenology of Perception* (New York: Humanities), Chap. IX.

The object of this unselfish existence is the person; the immediate source of this call is also the person. This call is rooted in the autonomous value of the person as such, a value of which we are aware as soon as we express this call in our life, in every genuine encounter, in every genuine dialogue. This call, which makes itself heard unmistakably in encounter and intersubjectivity, is a basic phenomenon of the human experience. It constitutes the moral experience. All moral demands are nothing but expressions and interpretations of this basic demand, though adjusted to the various situations of human life.

These situations are complex patterns of life. They show aspects that are universally human and apply to all ages because they make up the human condition as such. They also show features common to the historic phase in which we live. Lastly, they show strictly personal features that are peculiar to my life, my circumstances, my vocation, my potentialities, my responsibilities, my most intimate history. But these three aspects cannot be separated. I do not live in three situations: a general human condition, a social situation of this age and a personal situation. These three are one. The contemporary situation is the contemporary pattern of the general human condition and my individual situation is the concrete pattern that the contemporary situation assumes in my life. My personal situation embraces the contemporary situation at its most concrete, just as this contemporary situation is the concrete and historical expression of the human condition at large. The situation in which I must decide my moral orientation and my duty of the moment, is therefore ultimately a personal situation which is inescapably my own.

Just as there is but one situation, so there is but one morality: I do not subscribe to three moralities but to one only, and this morality is the norm for my personal life, however much it incorporates general norms derived from the general human or the contemporary situation. As Newman says, following the *Nichomachean Ethics*, every man must make his own moral norms and follow them. This is not laxity or lack of clarity or relativism in moral matters. It does not unsettle morality; it does not open an

escape hatch to get rid of, let us say, the great prohibitions of the
ten commandments; but it breaks through the fixation of morality.
Morality becomes personal and dynamic, and so loses its oppressive negative quality. It becomes a positive and inspiring *élan* upward, toward a greater humanity. It does not stand over me with a
constant "You may not do this, you may not do that", but it wells
up within me with power and zest and says, "I must, I will, I shall".
The face of morality has changed. The sorrowful frowning negative headshake is replaced by a glad and positive acceptance, which
expresses our growth toward generosity and love.

It should, then, be obvious that this positive and personalist
morality is no less demanding than a general morality or a social
convention. On the contrary, it asks constantly more, or rather,
as we become more free, more human, and realize more fully the
task of being a person, we shall obviously make constantly higher
demands on our generosity.

All this follows logically from the basic principle that the source
of true morality lies in the conscience, *i.e.*, in our freedom as essentially called upon to make us abandon our self and grow toward
generosity and unselfishness. This is the dynamic element in morality. What may be a duty for me is perhaps not a duty for another,
because our situations differ, and these situations imply the degree
of moral maturity and autonomy that we have reached individually. One cannot impose heroism, but every man can get into a
situation which demands an heroic decision according to his moral
judgment. Authentic personalist morality is therefore by nature
dynamic, open, growing in the breadth and intensity of its demands, and differing according to the individual.

That this personalist morality, individually different, and finding
its norm in the autonomous value of the person, expresses the
moral tendency of our age needs no long argument. We want to
escape from a static group morality in order to reach an authentic
morality of the human person. The kind of moral consciousness
shown by the true *élite* of today can be seen in the emphasis on
the inviolate dignity of the human person; in the affirmation of
universal equality and brotherhood; in the fight for human rights

throughout the world; in the movements to break down the walls between religions, classes, races and cultures and to reach a level at which man speaks to man as equal to equal.

But I want to stress the personal and subjective conditions that are required to make this breakthrough of genuine morality real and effective. These modern tendencies will remain wishful thinking and abstract ideas if they are not embodied in a growing number of leading personalities who have realized all this in their own lives. This breakthrough will only grow in the measure in which it is realized by persons who have overcome their selfishness sufficiently to live their human existence as an existence for other people.

I have tried to deal philosophically with the ideal and demands of this personalist morality. In fact, these philosophical thoughts were clarified and guided by Christian thought that goes back to the revelation of humanity in the manhood of Jesus Christ. I do not wish to go into the question of whether philosophy by itself can discover this ideal and define it. It is certain that Jesus himself and the Gospel have revealed to us the possibility of living for others. What appears to every man as an anonymous and wished-for ideal has been given a name in Jesus Christ, and with it the guarantee that realization is possible.

In the revelation of God's love toward us and the world, we have received the power to love others as he loved us. Christ's love is not only the great exemplar but also the source of that genuine morality of which I have spoken. Since the incarnation there has been no opposition and hardly a distinction between the search for God and the search for human happiness. Whoever takes to heart the great concerns of this world may be certain that he not only loves man and the world, but God himself.

Joseph T. C. Arntz, O. P. / *Zwolle, Netherlands*

Natural Law and Its History

In 1947 Heinrich Rommen wrote a small book entitled *Die ewige Wiederkehr des Naturrechts*.[1] The way in which this natural law keeps on turning up again and again made him conclude that man apparently cannot do without it. But the more this need is felt, the more puzzling is the fact that the concept of natural law just as constantly disappears. There are obviously periods when it flourishes and others when it declines. The teaching of it has a history. What kind of history? Does it reveal itself in this history? And has this any consequences for man?

To find the answers to these questions I shall first deal with the two peaks of its historical development, Stoicism (I) and St. Thomas Aquinas (II). Then we must see how this history affects us (III), and finally, an attempt will be made to arrive at a solution, a new theory (IV).

I

STOICISM

The history of the concept of natural law begins in ancient Greece, and, curiously enough, with a contrast between what is

[1] H. Rommen, *Die ewige Wiederkehr des Naturrechts*, 2nd ed. (Münster, 1947); see *idem*, *Natural Law* (Herder, 1947).

physei dikaion and what is *nomô dikaion*.[2] A distinction was made between what is just "by nature" and what by force of law. What was just by nature was called the unwritten law.

At first, the meaning of "by nature" was very vague. It was not a technical term of philosophy, and corresponded to "by itself", "obviously", or "naturally", in modern parlance. It contained no declaration about a possible general and unchangeable nature in the philosophical sense. Moreover, the contrast between *physei* and *nomô* lies within the scope of human law and is therefore of human concern.

The Greek view of the world, however, contained a feature that tended to eliminate this contrast between *physei* and *nomô*. To the Greek, the world in which he had his being was a *cosmos*, an ordered and harmonious whole, which, in turn, pointed to an idea. Plato made this explicit by maintaining that what was beautiful in this world could lead to the Idea of the Beautiful. Aristotle saw in "the work of nature the work of an intelligence". The Stoics expressed this by saying that a divine Logos permeated the universe, and that man shares in this Logos in a special way.[3]

By assuming an immanent Logos in nature and in man, the Stoics canceled out the difference between nature and reason in principle. For the Stoic thinker, to act according to reason and to act according to nature are identical. And since the law is the product of reason, law and nature are united, and henceforth, we can talk of a "natural law".[4] But by natural law one can mean two things: the cosmic order of the universe, and that principle in every individual being, whereby it fits into this great universe: its "nature". The cosmic order and the nature of things are both assumed to be unchangeable. As such, they give expression to an eternal law.

The Stoic synthesis indeed eliminates a contrast. The question is whether both elements have been suitably united. Stoic thought itself already shows a certain discord that points to a flaw: Ancient

[2] Aristotle, *Nichomachean Ethics*, Bk. 5, c. 10, 1134b 18–21.

[3] J. Stelzenberger, *Die Beziehungen der frühchristlichen Sittenlehre zur Ethik der Stoa* (Munich, 1933), p. 100.

[4] Stelzenberger, *op. cit.*, p. 104.

Stoicism (322–204 B.C.) puts the stress on nature, the objective element, while Middle Stoicism (2nd–1st century B.C.) puts it rather on human reason, the subjective element. Both elements can still be reconciled in the Logos, but this means basically: outside ourselves, in the all-embracing Logos.

This takes us back to the prehistory of the teaching on natural law. The idea that the world is a cosmos is nothing but the rationalization of an archaic religious attitude toward life, an attempt at explaining the mystery of nature. When man admires nature, he already has that philosophical sense of wonder that tries to penetrate to the principle of this cosmic order, the teleological principle as the formal and final cause, a Logos that, as the efficient cause of nature, gives natural order its sacred character.

When seen against this background it is clear why the early Stoic tradition in particular has lived on in history. Ulpian, the famous Roman jurist (d. 228 A.D.), broke up this synthesis. He made a distinction between a *ius naturale*, which reigns in the animal world (*quod omnia animalia docuit*), and a *ius gentium*, which reigns in the world of human beings, as opposed to animals (*quo gentes humanae utuntur, solis hominibus inter se commune*).[5] A flaw has appeared in the all-embracing cosmic order. "Natural law" (*ius naturale*) belongs to the non-human sector of the cosmos.

The period when Stoic philosophy was still flourishing saw the advent of Christianity. Insofar as our problem is concerned, this brought in three new elements: the question of the *Decalogue*, Paul's *Letter to the Romans* and the *Prologue to St. John*.

The Question of the Decalogue

Jesus says that he has not come to abolish the law, but to fulfill it. The Christian community understood this as meaning that it is not bound either to the ceremonial or the juridical precepts of the Old Testament but only to the decalogue. And, like the message of salvation, this decalogue has, therefore, universal significance.

[5] J. M. Aubert, *Le droit romain dans l'oeuvre de Saint Thomas* (Bibliotèque thomiste, 30, Paris, 1955), p. 93.

Later theology will consequently study the question of the relationship between the decalogue and natural law.[6]

The Letter to the Romans

When Paul began to preach the Gospel to hellenized Roman society, he adopted the language of that environment. The literary character of the first chapters of the *Letter to the Romans* is that of Stoic disputation. In that context occur the words: "When Gentiles who have no [Mosaic] law do by nature [*physei*] what the Law prescribes, these having no law are a law unto themselves" (Rom. 2, 14). These words led Christian thought to adopt the Stoic teaching on natural law. If one wonders whether this is a legitimate induction, one ought in any case to remember that Paul does not refer to professional philosophy but to its popularized form.[7]

The Prologue to St. John

Exegetically the Prologue carries on the Old Testament thought of God creating through his eternal Word. Augustine links this thought with the Platonic-Stoic idea of the eternal law, and also with the concept of natural law in Romans 2, 14.[8] In fact, this means a reinforcing of the idea that the teleological order in nature expresses God's purpose and has, therefore, a normative value. Thus, the early Christian tradition carries on the philosophical tradition of the Stoics.

II

ST. THOMAS AQUINAS

When in the 13th century the great attempts were made to organize systematic theology into a major synthesis, there were four main elements in the field, whose mutual relations had to be defined: eternal law, natural law, the *ius gentium* and the decalogue. It was the great merit of William of Auxerre that he linked the

[6] Stelzenberger, *op. cit.*, pp. 120ff.; O. Lottin, *Psychologie et morale aux XIIe et XIIIe siècles* (Louvain, 1948), Vol. II, 1, pp. 75 and 87.

[7] Stelzenberger, *op. cit.*, p. 114.

[8] A. Schubert, *Augustins Lex Aeterna-Lehre nach Inhalt und Quellen* (*Beiträge*, XXIV, 2) (Münster, 1924).

natural moral sense in man with the first principles of speculative reason.[9] This underlies St. Thomas' explanation.

St. Thomas deals with the natural law *ex professo* in his treatise on law (Ia IIae, qq. 90–108). This treatise is related to theology from the start. It opens with "God who instructs us through the law",[10] and finishes with a discussion of the new law.[11]

The first question of the treatise contains the well-known definition of law by its causes: the law is an ordinance of reason, tending toward the common good, promulgated by him who is in charge of the community.[12] St. Thomas maintains consistently that law is an ordinance of reason, and therefore a product of reason. This rational character of the law is the basis for a distinction we shall meet with in a moment: the law properly so called, and the law not properly so called.[13]

The next question deals with the variety of law—not with different kinds of law as if there were a kind of genus-species relationship between the law in general and particular laws. The term is used analogously in different cases. To ignore this analogous use of the term leads to legalism in matters of morality.

Two of these different concepts of law must be dealt with in detail: eternal law and natural law. According to St. Thomas, natural law must be defined as a participation of the eternal law.

As has been said, the Stoics identified eternal law with the eternal order in the nature of things. It is a cosmic value. But for St. Thomas eternal law is identical with God's being, his ideas, his providence and his government of the world.[14] This means that the world is governed by God's eternal wisdom. Whatever is found in creation is but a participation in eternal law.[15] Taken strictly, this leaves wide open the question whether this order can change or not.

Cosmic reality, then, participates in the eternal law. But this

[9] Lottin, *op. cit.*, pp. 75–6.
[10] Ia IIae, q. 90, prooemium.
[11] Ia IIae, q. 108.
[12] Ia IIae, q. 90, a. 4.
[13] Ia IIae, q. 90, a. 1 ad 2; q. 91, a. 2 ad 3.
[14] Ia IIae, q. 91, a. 2 ad 1.
[15] *Idem*, in corp.

participation is expressed in two ways. Irrational beings participate in this eternal law insofar as they are directed toward their end by their nature. In this case, "law", which coincides with their nature, is used in a metaphorical sense. Man, however, participates in the eternal law through his reason: "The light of natural reason, whereby we discern what is good and what is evil, which is the function of the natural law, is nothing but an imprint on us of the Divine light."[16] Natural law, therefore, is nothing but the rational creature's participation in eternal law.

Note the expression "the light of natural reason". Its meaning is indicated in the *ad 2* of the same article: "Every act of reason and will in us is derived (*derivatur*, which is different from a logical deduction) from that which is according to nature. For all reasoning is derived from principles that are known naturally, and all striving that leads to the end in view is derived from our natural striving toward the last end." Natural reason is therefore directed toward what is known "by nature". In other words, it is directed toward what reason cannot ignore without denying itself. The connection between knowledge and what is known is so close that one can find in St. Thomas texts that seem to refer to an innate knowledge.[17] We may, therefore, conclude that the contents of natural law is what man knows by nature.

Thomas maintains his position when he has to answer the question, what are the commandments of natural law. The real purpose of this question is clearer in the usual, though not original, heading of the article: "Whether the Natural Law Contains Several Precepts, or One Only?" [18] In answering this question Thomas makes use of Aristotle's view of science (in the broadest sense), which is a

[16] *Ibid.*

[17] *De Veritate* 10, 6 ad 6; 11, 1 ad 5; II *Sent.*, dist. XXIV, 2, 3; I, 18, 3. See also expressions such as "Imprint of the divine light in us" (Ia IIae, q. 91, a. 2); "The light of Reason" (II *Sent.*, dist. XLII, 1, 4 ad 3; "The light of reason divinely set within, by which God speaks within us" (*De Veritate*, 11, 1, ad 13); "The light of this sort of reason, by which principles of this sort are known to us, is placed in us by God as a sort of likeness of uncreated truth resulting in us" (*De Veritate* 11, 1); "The intrinsic principle of knowledge . . . is in us by God" (*Contra Gent.* II, 75). Quotations from P. M. van Overbeke, "Loi naturel et droit naturel selon S. Thomas," in *Revue Thomiste* 57 (1957), p. 75.

[18] Ia IIae, q. 94, a. 2.

habitus conclusionum (a habit of drawing conclusions), starting from principles that are basic, true and immediately known. With these principles the predicate follows the subject without a middle term, because the predicate is included in the definition of the subject, or because the subject is incorporated in the definition of the predicate. This is the formal aspect. Insofar as the material aspect is concerned, some concepts are simply common property, others are only known to scholars. Hence the distinction between such expressions as "immediately evident in themselves" or "evident to all", and, on the other hand, "what is evident in itself". But in practice, only scholars are concerned with this distinction. From these principles anyone can draw the more obvious conclusions, but scholars can derive further conclusions from them.

This schema sounds very dull and scholastic, but it has been very useful to St. Thomas, and it will prove more fruitful than appears at first sight. The first advantage was that it became possible to sort out the various elements of tradition: natural law has to do with the first insights of practical reason, while the decalogue covers the field of derived conclusions.[19]

The second advantage was that, in this perspective, it became possible to arrive at a coherent doctrine of natural law. The more widely one extends natural law, the more difficult it becomes to maintain that it is one and the same for all men, known at all times and in all places, always valid, and never to be erased from men's hearts.[20] All this is only true, according to St. Thomas, for natural law in the strictest sense: the most general principles are really intelligible to everybody without more ado, such as, that good must be done and evil avoided,[21] which comes to the same thing as acting rationally.[22] This enables St. Thomas to hold on to his *naturaliter cognitum et volitum* (that which is naturally known and willed).

[19] Ia IIae, q. 100, a. 3 ad 1.
[20] Ia IIae, q. 94, a. 4–6.
[21] Ia IIae, q. 94, a. 2.
[22] According to C. Anderson, "De natuurwet," in *Werkgenootschap van katholieke theologen in Nederland* (1960), p. 134, the following items do not fall under natural law in St. Thomas' view: idolatry, blasphemy, false teaching, the respect due to old age and to the State, usury and prostitution.

It would, however, be wrong to limit natural law to these two formal principles. Thomas develops what it is toward which man is inclined by nature (Ia IIae, q. 94, a. 2). Here he uses the above mentioned distinction of Ulpian. Why he does this is clear enough. He returns to the doctrine of natural inclinations in order to give some substance to that "good-to-be-done" and to show to what this rational behavior must be applied. We shall see in a moment that this return to the natural inclinations threatened to become fatal to his own vision. Let us first sum up St. Thomas' own view. He accepts the existence of natural law. It is participation in the eternal law by the rational creature as such. But it is most properly concerned with what is known by nature, and in this sense it is identical for all and always valid.

Before going on from here, we should have a brief look at the development of natural law after St. Thomas.

From what has been said it is clear that St. Thomas' view lies wholly in the line of Aristotle's intellectualism. This explains why a nominalistic and voluntaristic reaction set in. This reaction finally led to that theonomous, positivistic morality (God has positively decreed all moral laws), which denied natural law by implication. This was a complete rejection of St. Thomas' synthesis.

For our present purpose, however, two other tendencies are more important. Reaction to this voluntarism easily led again to rationalism, and the challenge contained in the use of Aristotle's teaching on science is readily accepted. Attempts are made to construct a purely deductive science of morality. What is worse: everything that can be deduced by close argument from given premises is counted as natural law,[23] as long as one remembers

---

[23] I hope it is clear that I have in mind here both the late scholastic teaching on natural law in the field of international law, and the German teaching on natural law of the school of Puffendorf and Wolff. That some Thomists were also inclined this way is shown by Bañez in II IIae, q. 57, a. 3, who says: "Everything gathered by a good conscience from moral principles is the natural law." Similarly Sylvius, in Ia IIae, q. 94, a. 2, where he says: "I answer that both principles and conclusions drawn from the principles belong to the natural law . . . whether it tends to something directly or by means of nature, this is to be considered as belonging to the law of nature, if it be such that it follows of necessity from nature and actual principles and

that the farther the conclusions are from the premises, the more limited will be their universal validity. Such distant conclusions will need confirmation by positive law to have any real validity.[24] In other words, when natural law is stretched too far, it turns into positive law. This process is obviously alien to natural law.

Another theological tradition could be considered to have developed from St. Thomas' teaching on natural inclinations insofar as these inclinations tend toward man's final end. This development implies that man participates in eternal law in two ways: at the irrational level and at the rational one. I doubt whether such a way of looking at the problem can be called Thomistic. Whatever we call it, there is a theology of natural law that considers man's physical nature as normative. It appears in every kind of medical and sexual moral argument. I must add here that what is paramount in St. Thomas' view, namely, the question of intelligibility, plays no part in this kind of theology. What for him was of secondary importance, namely, *quod natura omnia animalia docuit*, predominates here. Ultimately this means that in the case of man natural law in the metaphorical sense would have priority over natural law in the strict sense. This is no longer St. Thomas, but a return to Stoicism where man as such disappears.

III

How This History Affects Us

When, after this hasty survey, we return to the real sense of St. Thomas' view, we notice two things. In Stoicism the accent falls on nature, in St. Thomas on man. For the Stoics the opposition between nature and reason is eliminated by the immanence of the Logos; for St. Thomas the contrast is bridged by reason, human

---

it obliges by force of natural reason alone, without any positive ordinance, divine or human." St. Thomas' text in the following footnote obviously escaped the attention of this author.

[24] "Those things that natural law teaches as derived from the first principles of the law of nature, do not have coactive force absolutely by way of precept unless sanctioned by divine or human law," says St. Thomas in IV *Sent.*, dist. XXXIII, q. 1, a. 1 ad 2.

reason. For him it is the *naturaliter cognitum* (what is naturally known) that matters. For us, so many centuries later in the history of philosophy, this opposition already shows the seed of the priority of the object over the priority of the subject. Let us look for a moment at both views in this light.

If nature is taken as normative, this presupposes a definite attitude toward nature and the possibility of seeing in it a miracle of intelligence. It is the attitude of philosophical wonder developed into *theoria*, a concrete vision. But this attitude rests on a habit that appeals to what is constant in things and that presents man as knowing what these constant elements are. The world is a mirror, but we do not yet know that it reflects ourselves because we do not yet know that it is we ourselves who make these constant elements appear in nature. Man faces the existing order of things in which he feels safe, as *das Unwesentliche* (the unreal).

If this order is present in nature, also without man, then it has to be the work of an all-embracing intelligence, of a divine orderer of the world. But we have become aware of the fact that God is not such an "orderer", a kind of superior skilled laborer. This is an anthropomorphic conception that turns God into a world-size "maker". Not knowing any other Logos than a manufacturing Logos, the Stoics were consistent in making the Logos immanent in the world, and so the Logos becomes *das Unwesentliche* (the unreal). We should turn Hegel's words about nature: the Logos "is nature outside itself" (*ist die Natur im Äusser-sich-sein*). This is the most appropriate expression for *natura artis magistra* (nature is the teacher of art), which is here enlarged to become *ordo quam ratio facit in operibus voluntatis* (the order that nature produces in the operations of the will).[25]

To offset this, St. Thomas puts the full emphasis on human reason. The contrast between nature and reason is lifted by the *naturaliter cognitum* (what is naturally known), which is the key point. But this implies the question, what kind of role, then, is still to be played by reality? This implies another question: what is the significance of St. Thomas' realism for his concept of natural

[25] St. Thomas, *In X Libros Ethicorum*, Liber I, lect. 1, n. 1.

law? It would not arise if he had not known the temptation of idealism in this matter. This temptation is inherent in every philosophy based on the subject.

The first article of the question on natural law already shows St. Thomas in line with this type of philosophy. The controversial question of whether natural law is a *habitus* or the *synderesis*,[26] conceals another one: is natural law something made by reason? The point here is not whether a given definition of the law is applicable, but it concerns man's own expression of the view that, only in this way, natural law is binding on man. In other words, the point is the development of the thought that "the rational creature is subject to divine providence in the most excellent way, insofar as it partakes of a share of providence, by being provident both for itself and for others".[27] What is in question, therefore, is the recognition of man as a subject, determining his own natural law for himself.

St. Thomas' inclination to the theory of innate knowledge shows that he was not immune from the temptation of idealism. Innate ideas express the subject's independence as opposed to the world. His version of this shows an affinity with Kant. He is concerned with the *principia communissima*, and this means those principles that are contained in man's action, at whatever level. These principles are thus formal principles within the scope of man's reflection.

What separates St. Thomas from Kant is that for St. Thomas these principles appear in the action itself, not in the explicit reflection on the nature of this action, on goodwill. The first practical principles, too, are for him the fruit of experience. It is therefore basically his realism that divides him from Kant. The difficulty is how to square this realistic aspect with his "subject" philosophy.

The historical development of Thomism as outlined above shows this difficulty in the concrete. There were two tendencies. The one

[26] Ia IIae, q. 94, a. 1. This article is aimed against Peter of Tarantaise. See Lottin, *op. cit.*, p. 94.
[27] Ia IIae, q. 91, a. 2.

started from the first practical principles to arrive at a system of natural law that would be valid always and everywhere, and would therefore stand as much outside history as the principle itself. We have already seen that this purely deductive procedure ends up by turning natural law into positive law. It means that this indefinite perpetuation of analysis and deduction has lost touch with concrete reality. In spite of the realistic start of this system the reality becomes unreal to it because it rests on ideas. That an idea should spring from experience seems unrealistic to one who relies exclusively on ideas. This betrays a view of man as a being for whom thought is more essential than nature. This shows that man and nature cannot be measured by the same standards.

The other tendency meant to be radically realistic. Natural inclinations set the norm and all that man has to do is accept them. This makes the rational element unreal and realism degenerates into physicism. Man remains part of nature.

It is not astonishing that Thomism has known both these developments, when we look at it now. It reflects an ambiguity in St. Thomas' own philosophy. Nor could he easily have avoided it. Historically he stands halfway between the Stoic *natura artis magistra* and the contemporary *natura artis materia*.[28] This historical development not only implies a changed view of nature, but also of man. Contact with the world around him makes man conscious of his reason. In this consciousness he perceives the ideal of the pure *theoria* and sees himself as "subject" as opposed to "nature". Insofar as a genuine and profound intervention in nature still escapes him, this nature is still a stable factor for him. It has not yet become *artis materia*, and man does not yet see himself in the fullness of his power over nature. This means that he does not yet fully see himself as "subject".

For our purpose this leads to two conclusions. Man is a being that becomes fully conscious of himself through his relation to nature and to others. This implies that we cannot neglect our im-

[28] Cf. J. J. Loeff, "Het naturrecht en de ontwikkeling van het ethisch denken," in *Sociale Wetenschappen* 2 (1959), pp. 1–50, *passim*. See also M. G. Plattel, "Situatie-ethiek en Natur wet," in *Sociale Wetenschappen* 3 (1960), pp. 265–92, *passim*.

mediately surrounding reality lest we fall victim to one or another illusion unconnected with the world. The second conclusion is that man's relation to himself, nature and the others is apparently no longer a constant element. This introduces a historical dimension into our "self" as object. It is, therefore, not only true that the teaching on natural law has a history. Natural law itself becomes history.

IV
SOLUTION

These conclusions point a way toward a solution, which is to adopt neither Stoicism nor St. Thomas without qualification. If the starting point is an unchangeable nature, then all that is left is a change in our knowledge of this unchangeable fact. If we start with St. Thomas' first principles, then the development is simply the history of their explication. But this history cannot touch these first principles in themselves. We must look in another direction; we must return to the origin of these first principles, and not at the level of reflection, but at the level of the evidence that precedes all reflection, and that is only expressed in judgment. In other words, is there anything which is both evident and imposes itself categorically?

All things that appear, appear only insofar as I let them. It is my attention that pulls them out of the background and lets them fall back again. My freedom, however, can do nothing about the fact that something shows itself. "An immense individual asserts itself," says Merleau-Ponty. But this is not all: "Every existence understands itself and understands the others".[29] The appearing (the phenomena) of the world and the others are basic facts, and we understand our own being as a being related to others and to the world.

The others appear (show themselves) to us primarily in com-

[29] M. Merleau-Ponty, *Phénoménologie de la Perception* (Paris, 1945), p. 468; see *idem*, *Phenomenology of Perception* (New York: Humanities).

munication. This means that the world about which I speak appears as "together with . . ." or rather, as "shared with . . .". The ellipsis should suggest that the fact of communication draws a vague but definite line in that "immense individual which asserts itself" between what I speak about and those to whom I speak. Communication includes a vague awareness of the wholly individual existence of the other, without coming explicitly to the surface.

In principle this concludes the matter. If the primary and "original" evidence only showed the presence of the world, there would be no chance of subjects appearing within this world. Sartre proved this conclusively against Heidegger.[30] But others, too, appear to me in precisely their own existence. This is communicating. Communication proves to me that they are there, without making explicit *what* they are and without anticipating any explicit awareness that they and I have of our existence. This means two things. First, there is a primary evidence that lends itself to explicitness. Secondly, in this explicitness, man, "in and for himself", becomes what he is. It only remains to trace this explicitness.

This explicitness is formal in character. For the sake of clarity I want to say something first about its contents.

The question is to find something that will help us to understand the factual multiplicity of cultures. These are always the realization of human possibilities that emerge from a specific view of man. But the principle must also be able to explain—although this is not our concern here—that some cultures show an endlessly repetitive pattern while others develop and reach a ceiling above which they cannot rise, and that our own culture appears to us as having infinite tasks in front of it that betray one and the same inspiration.

This inspiration or leading principle is for us respect for the other as subject. But this has already a long history, showing three lines of development. The first is from a confused statement of this principle to a constantly clearer perception. To illustrate this: the

---

[30] J. P. Sartre, *L'Etre et le Néant* (Paris, 1943), pp. 301ff.; see *idem, Being and Nothingness* (New York: Citadel, 1964).

development from "respect for blood relationship" to respect for the human subject, even the unborn or even the possible subject (birth control as respect for the right to suitable education, whether this will happen or not). The second line is the universal extension of the other's recognition as subject: tribal ethics that expand into universal ethics, not fully realized as long as there is still discrimination of any kind, and this will remain for as long as we still live "sous le régime de la rareté".[31] The third line is the increasingly radical recognition of the other. Again, by way of illustration: the increasing respect for the other's life, for his possessions, and, purely as an example, for the mystery he is.

While all this is not yet by any means a reality, we experience today the fact that something completely new is going to happen. In the problems put to us by the study of "situation ethics", it is not only a matter of man as subject, but as unique subject.

The bearing of this last point becomes clearer when we realize that this recognition of the other has its reverse in that we must no longer look on man as a "thing". At first, man is but a "something", is treated as "something" and treats others as "something". Only in history he discovers what he is, or rather, in history he develops himself into what he is. It is not as if from the beginning man was rational enough "in himself", but not yet "for himself". In the beginning his rationality was no more than one of his potentialities. When he discovers his rationality, he becomes aware of the fact that he does not exist by the same standards as the sub-human. In the discovery of his being unique he also discovers that the yardstick of his existence does not apply to others, although the difference is not clearly perceived.

When we try to express this in philosophical terms we get the following: there is primary evidence that we live with others. But this is an abstraction. In fact, we live with others according to one or other set of mores, or ethos. This ethos is "livable"; otherwise, this living together according to this ethos would simply disintegrate. This implies that it is based on a real aspect of man, and contains in itself a view of man and of the world. Insofar as man

[31] *Idem, Critique de la Raison Dialectique* (Paris, 1960), pp. 205 and 225.

stands in need of evidence, we must say that any basic pattern of life always contains its own evidence, which remains valid while the pattern remains valid, but will be doubted when the pattern itself is called in question. Supported by evidence that is at least hypothetically unshakable, every ethos tends toward self-continuation.

But in every ethos there also lies a tendency toward development. This does not mean that it does develop in fact, nor that it can develop indefinitely. But this point falls outside our argument. Here we are looking for an *a priori* condition that makes evolution possible. This condition we see in the tension between the fact of living together and the manner of living together. Just as there can be bad faith in the individual's relation to the other when he treats this other at the same time as object and as subject,[32] so there can be bad faith in an ethos. A simple example is racialism. Every notice, "No Negroes allowed", recognizes the Negro as man by the very fact of the prohibition, and at the same time denies him what is his due. Put in a more abstract way: the world pattern contained in an ethos can, among all those who live together, favor some, so that they alone can live fully together, and use others. Such an ambiguity has to be removed. The first conclusion of this argument is that "living together" is no longer an abstract expression, but is becoming a truth in the Hegelian sense of the word,[33] and so an ideal norm to which the factual living together must conform.

This evolution can only come about when we have become aware of the tension that exists and the way in which it can be relieved. This awareness of the tension can be stimulated by prophetic wit-

[32] Cf. Sartre's explanation of the concrete relationships with the other in *L'Etre et le Néant*, pp. 428–84. These must be understood as descriptions of attitudes of "bad faith". The term is used in the text in Sartre's sense.

[33] By way of illustration we might say: The reality is "to have written this article in the Dutch language as it was in 1964, with its own choice of words, style," etc. Dutch is the *truth* of this article, which makes it comprehensible. But in its turn Dutch is also the *reality* when compared with the Teutonic languages. These, too, are both truth and reality. And so we can go on until we reach something that is only truth, and contains the ultimate implications and sense of all reality within that scope.

ness, but the tension can also be clearly seen when there is a rift between the way in which man is shown in the ethos, and the way in which he is shown in his relation to nature. Hegel's categories of lord and slave[34] can serve as an example of this dichotomy. At the level of "living together" he sees himself and is seen by others as powerless. At the level of labor he sees himself as powerful. This ambiguity can be one of the motive forces in the ethical evolution.

The direction that this evolution will take should be clear from what has been said. The first thing to go should be any form of discrimination so that the ethos may at least extend to all members of the group. It is true that this universality is even then only apparent, but it is a necessary stage on the road to true universality.

The knowledge of this true universality spreads through practical conduct, at least in our Western culture. In his constant association with things man learns by experience that they have certain constant qualities, a nature, which is always and everywhere the same. In absorbing this fact, man realizes that he himself, too, has a nature. Psycho-physical nature prompts man to realize this but his true nature is nothing but his potentiality to know the universal: his rationality. This is, therefore, a potentiality in him that grows in and through the practice of living.

As he becomes aware of his rationality, man discerns the foundation of an ethos that can make this applicable to human "living together" directly and without more ado. This ethos is then based on the universal nature of man, and makes him realize that all have the same rights and duties. Thus natural law develops.

If the ethos became coextensive with his truth, the opposition between reality and truth would vanish. Truth would then be nothing but a reality that has become conscious of itself as a universal communication of all subjects, a communication that has consciously developed its own shape. In this process communication shows its own true character. It is a communication between rational subjects who have become conscious *an und für sich* (in

[34] G. W. F. Hegel, *Phänomenologie des Geistes*, Hoffmeister, ed. (Leipzig, 1937), pp. 144ff.

and for themselves) of the fact that they are able to communicate because they are able to act rationally.

For the time being, however, the disappearance of this opposition is but an ideal. The actual achievement of this universal recognition would amount to the achievement of Kant's *Reich der Zwecke* (the kingdom of purpose). And this would also abolish the opposition to the *Reich der Natur* (the kingdom of nature) because nature would be subjected completely to the service of man. And this, in turn, would abolish the kingdom of scarcity and poverty.

This ideal unity of truth and reality would, however, be doomed to disintegration, and it is worth thinking about this, because it exposes the fact that this unity is presupposed. By making rationality identical with human nature, we can seize it, and in this way it can give shape to a law that applies to all rational creatures in the same way. But by concentrating on rationality as such, we put it beyond the pale of every other created factor. For, as a rational being, man creates his own possibilities and realizes himself through these possibilities. He is, for himself, "the being of endless tasks". He achieves himself in each of these tasks. Thus he is not only master of nature at large, but also master of *his* nature.

Would this not mean the abolition of natural law? Perhaps it does, but in a very special sense. We have already seen that natural law is not a goal, and that, in fact, a totally new concept of man is beginning to take shape. An abolition of natural law in Hegel's sense (overcoming, fulfillment) is something very different from writing off natural law as out-of-date. It means that natural law has met its truth insofar as we realize that natural law is nothing but the truth of "living together". Natural law is itself the primary evidence that makes itself explicit constantly, and constantly demands to be translated into concrete human relationships. It is the motive force that drives us to give their full human value to all the relationships as they appear within the scope of man's concept of himself at any particular moment. This humanizing process is not arbitrary, but guided and borne by this primary evidence.

If natural law itself is called to achieve its own truth, and at the same time to make itself more explicit and to incarnate itself, it is a historical process. Insofar as this primary evidence imposes itself, natural law is also the motive force in this process, a motive force which "moves as an object of desire moves" (*kinei ôs erômenon,*[35] as goodness and truth move.

[35] Aristotle, *XII Metaph.*, c. 7, Bekker, ed., 1072, b 3.

Gerhard J. Botterweck/*Bonn, W. Germany*

The Form and Growth of the Decalogue

I

KINDS OF LAW IN THE OLD TESTAMENT

In a basic study on the origins of Israelite law[1] Albrecht Alt distinguished two different kinds of law: case law and statutory law. Case law usually has a conditional sentence in the third person, with a statement of the case (protasis) and a judicial conclusion (apodosis), as, for instance, in Exodus 22, 16f.: "If a man seduces a virgin who is not betrothed, and lies with her, he shall pay her marriage price and marry her. If her father refuses to give her to him, he must still pay the customary marriage price for virgins." This type of law covers slaves, blood-relationship, marriage, wounding, property, etc. These cases belong to everyday life and fall under the lay jurisdiction of the Torah.[2] Neither from the point of view of the people nor from that of religion is there anything specifically Israelite about these cases. They are common to the general condition of the law in the ancient East and in the age before Israel. It is therefore probable that Israel took over this case law from the Canaanites when they occupied Palestine.

On the other hand, statutory law is usually formulated as a precept or a prohibition, most often in the second person singular,

[1] A. Alt, *Kleine Schriften zur Geschichte des Volkes Israel* I (1953), pp. 278–332.
[2] L. Koehler, *Die hebräische Rechtsgemeinde* (1931) in *Der hebräische Mensch* (1953), pp. 143–71.

and put in general groups (*e.g.*, the decalogue, Ex. 20; Deut. 5) or in specific groups (*e.g.*, the behavior of judges in Ex. 23, 6–9). This often takes the form of a decalogue or a dodecalogue and was originally in metrical style, for example: "You shall not repeat a false report. Do not join the wicked in putting your hand, as an unjust witness, upon anyone. Neither shall you allege the example of the many as an excuse for doing wrong . . ." (Ex. 23, 1ff.). According to Alt, this statutory law always ends in categorical prohibitions, whatever variety there may be in the expression;[3] moreover, all of it is typically Israelite and connected with Yahweh, even if the concise expression does not allow for an explicit mention of this.[4]

Under this heading of statutory law Alt also includes judicial statements or series with a participial construction, where the participial reference to the case is very closely linked with the sanction in the following verb. An example of this may be seen in the Sichemite dodecalogue of curses (Deut. 27, 15ff.): ". . . Cursed be he who dishonors his father or his mother! And all the people shall answer 'Amen!' " Alt equally includes the lists of crimes that deserve death (Ex. 21, 12. 15–17; 22, 18f.; 31, 14f.): "Whoever curses his father or mother shall be put to death" (Ex. 21, 17). Since this statutory law (including the participial form) has no parallel in ancient Eastern law, Alt tries to locate it in the specifically Israelite situation. This he finds in the proclamation of the statutory law at the feast of booths or tabernacles, every seventh year (Deut. 31, 10–13), and for the place, he looks to Sichem on the basis of Deuteronomy 27. The preliminaries for this development of statutory law were present "as soon as the bond with Yahweh was established between him and Israel, followed by the institution of the covenant and its renewal".[5]

The same author ranges the decalogue with this kind of statutory law, although in its original form it was probably prose rather than poetry. It is opposed to the special groups with a limited

[3] A. Alt, *op. cit.* I, p. 322.
[4] A. Alt, *op. cit.* I, p. 323.
[5] A. Alt, *op. cit.* I, p. 330.

purpose because it clearly means to embrace all; it mentions no penalties with its categorically stated prohibitions, and thus the juridical aspect yields in importance to the moral contents.[6]

Further investigation continued in the same direction as that laid down by Alt, while testing, modifying, correcting or completing particular points.

1. *A More Accurate Precision of Statutory Law*

In spite of the fact that Alt's definition of statutory law has been so widely accepted, the definition of "statutory" and "law" lacks precision. Both terms need to be differentiated and limited.

In its origin the formula of statutory law has no sequence of case and sanction, of how to establish the fact and what sanction to lay down; it rather expresses in a command or prohibition, in a valid and unconditional manner, whatever the legislator judges as just or unjust in the manifold relationships that bind his community together.[7] Insofar as there is no decision and sanction, this type of law does not suit the actual administration of justice and the decisions in concrete criminal cases; this demands case law which is much more practical with its varied ways of establishing the case or adjusting the sanction laid down in groups of precedents. One might say that many statutory formulas, even in the decalogue, convey a command or prohibition originally based on a detailed case; the prohibition of murder, for instance, is closely connected with the institution of blood vengeance, and theft may perhaps go back originally to the kidnapping of men, as one may guess from Exodus 21, 16: "A kidnaper, whether he steals his victim or still has him when caught, shall be put to death" (see also Deut. 24, 7). But even then the process of justice would still require a detailed specification of the circumstances of the

---

[6] A. Alt, *op. cit.* I, p. 322.

[7] Cf. R. Kilian, *Literarkritische und formgeschichtliche Untersuchung des Heiligkeitsgesetzes*, Diss. Masch. (1959), p. 11; *idem*, "Apodiktisches und kasuistisches Recht im Lichte ägyptischer Analogien," in *Biblische Zeitschrift* (1963), pp. 185–202, especially p. 189; H. Gese, "Beobachtungen zum Stil atl. Rechtsätze," in *Theologische Literaturzeitung* 85 (1960), pp. 147–50; E. Gerstenberger, *Wesen und Herkunft des sog. apodiktischen Rechts im A.T.* (1961), p. 34.

case, and its proper administration would still need the necessary sanction.

2. *The Juridical Formula in Participial Phrases and Adjectival Clauses*

Between the prohibition "You shall not kill" or the command "Honor your father and your mother" on the one hand, and the detailed formula of case law as in the law about slavery (Ex. 21, 2–11) on the other, there are the participial and adjectival clauses dealing with curses and capital crimes (Lev. 20, 9 . 10–18 . 20 . 21) and which Alt classifies as statutory. Insofar as these are concise and unconditional they approach the form of a prohibition or a command, but insofar as they carry the sanction of curse or death, they come close to case law. On closer inspection, however, both the participial phrase ("Whoever curses his father or mother . . ." in Exodus 21, 17) and the adjectival clause ("Anyone who curses his father or mother shall be put to death," in Leviticus 20, 9) specify the subject that deserves curse or death, and thus specify the case. But they differ from case law in the sanction ("curse", "death"). Does the text refer here to a real death penalty to be inflicted by the judicial community?[8] How and by whom should it be inflicted? It is obviously a matter of a magic death wish connected with sacred law,[9] and based on a proclamation of the divine will.

The same holds for expulsion from the community,[10] a kind of ritual and magic exile to safeguard certain taboos; the delinquent is driven out of the religious community. By way of example[11] one

[8] Thus, Alt, *op. cit.* I, p. 313; see also P. Van Imschoot, *Théologie de l'Anc. Test.* II (1956), p. 260.

[9] Cf. H. Cazelles, *Etudes sur le Code de l'Alliance* (1946), pp. 123f.; R. Kilian, *op. cit.* (Diss. Masch.), pp. 17 and 19.

[10] Cf. W. Zimmerli, "Die Eigenart der Prophetischen Rede des Ezechiel," in *Zeitschrift für die alttestamentische Wissenschaft* 66 (1954), pp. 1–26, especially pp. 13–19; *idem, Ezechiel. Bibl. Kommentar* (1957), pp. 303–9; R. Kilian, *Heiligkeitsgesetz* (1963), pp. 11f. According to Zimmerli, the formula is mainly inspired by "the punishment of man, pronounced by Yahweh himself . . . which can take place through a sudden divine intervention" (*op. cit.*, p. 304).

[11] The words in brackets may be a priestly revision of the original form. Cf. R. Kilian, *op. cit.*, (Diss. Masch.), p. 955.

may quote Leviticus 17, 3–4: "Any Israelite who slaughters an ox or a sheep or a goat, whether in the camp or outside of it, without first bringing it to the entrance of the Meeting Tent to present it as an offering to the Lord in front of his Dwelling, shall be judged guilty of bloodshed, and for this such a man shall be cut off from among his people." (See also Exodus 14, 6–11.)

Human administration of justice is hardly possible with the curse-and-blessing formulas[12] that are found linked with positive or negative commands (cf. Deut. 27, 11–13. 15ff.; Jos. 24, 25ff.; Deut. 28; Lev. 26). These formulas rather designate whoever has broken the basic laws about violence or religious taboos as the bearer of the curse which is immanent in the destructive power of evil. According to Deuteronomy 27, the community consents with its "Amen" to the expression of God's will and so identifies itself with the curse thus proclaimed. In the same way the blessing effects salvation and life for as long as the one blessed remains true to the proclaimed will of God in his behavior.

Therefore, the series of crimes that deserve to be cursed or to be punished by death are rightly detached from the strictly statutory series of positive and negative commands, and are understood as case-law formulas with a ritual slant, expressing the proclaimed will of God and the community. On the other hand, it would be wrong to take the participial clauses as "a concise imitation of the conditional sentence" [13] or to derive the more developed formulas of case law from the brief, metrical, serialized and orally transmitted key sentences of "case" judgment, as von Reventlow

---

[12] For the problem of curses and blessings, see J. Hempel, "Die israelitischen Anschauungen von Segen und Fluch im Lichte altorientalischer Paralelen," in Zeitschr. deutsch. morgenl. Ges. 79 (1925), pp. 20–110; M. Noth, "Die mit des Gesetzes Werken umgehen, die sind unter dem Fluch," in Von Bulnering-Festschrift (1938), pp. 127–45, also in (Gesammelte Studien 1957), pp. 155–71; J. Scharbert, " 'Fluchen' und 'Segnen' im A.T.," in Biblica 39 (1958), pp. 1–26; H. Junker, "Segen als heilsgschichtliches Motivwort im A.T.," in Sacra Pagina I (1959), pp. 548–58. Cf. also J. Pedersen, Israel: Its Life and Culture (1946), Vol. I, pp. 182–212, 411–52.

[13] H. Gese, "Beobachtungen zum Stil atl. Rechtsätze," in Theologisches Literaturzeitung 85 (1960), p. 148.

does.[14] Their meter, serialization, contents and ritual character distinguish them from the usual case-law formulas in the Torah where lay administration of justice is involved.[15] When the death curse is no longer properly understood later on, it is changed by an editorial reviser into stoning (Lev. 20, 2. 27, and elsewhere). Then the penalty of stoning is executed by the top layer of the community, the 'an hā'ārez, instead of being a divine punishment.[16]

Later I shall return to the question whether the positive and negative commands of the decalogue are linked with a kind of judicial decision in the formulas of curses or blessings in the context of a supervening composition such as the Sinai covenant.

II

STATUTORY LAW AND THE RELATIONS OF ISRAEL WITH GOD

The decalogue is introduced emphatically as a theophany and the promulgation of Yahweh's will by himself. Of the statutory series those mentioned in Exodus 22, 20ff.; 34, 12ff.; Leviticus 18–19 and Exodus 20, 2ff. belong to the great literary complex of the pericope dealing with Mount Sinai. Deuteronomy 5, 6ff. also refers to this, although here "the obvious and direct character of Yahweh's revelation is modified in favor of a message transmitted through Moses".[17] The connection of the negative command with a divine utterance or a direct entry upon the scene by Yahweh, etc., is mostly taken as proof of some link with cult, whether with the feast of the new year, or that of the tabernacles in Sichem, or some celebration of the covenant. Yet, one may wonder whether this connection is original or whether it only arose under the influence of some literary process; the connection with the Sinai pericope also needs investigation.

[14] Cf. "Kultisches Recht im A.T.," in *Zeitschrift für Theologie und Kirche* 60 (1963), pp. 268–304, especially p. 282.

[15] See also R. Kilian, *op. cit.* (Diss. Masch.), pp. 19f.

[16] Cf. A. Alt, *op. cit.* I, p. 313; H. von Reventlow and R. Kilian, *loc. cit.;* H. von Reventlow, *Kultisches Recht im A.T.*, p. 291.

[17] G. von Rad, *Das fünfte Buch Mose. Das Alte Test. Deutsch* (1964), p. 43.

1. Statutory Statements as Divine Utterance

The decalogue (Ex. 20, 2–17; Deut. 5, 5–22) opens with God's proclamation of himself,[18] "I, the Lord, am your God, who brought you out of the land of Egypt, that place of slavery" (Ex. 20, 2; Deut. 5, 6). With the expression "your God", which brings out the aspect of salvation history, Yahweh introduces himself into the presence of the listening community; according to Zimmerli this formula of God's self-presentation belongs to worship as it is used by the priest when he proclaims the law. But this presentation is at once linked with the deliverance of Israel from Egypt, which is part of salvation history. It is, however, curious that this divine First Person, "I", occurs only in the first two commandments, while the following commandments only mention Yahweh in the third person (Ex. 20, 10–12; Deut. 5, 11. 12. 15. 16). "Because both Yahweh's saving deeds and the divine law are proclaimed with reference to the introductory or concluding formula of Yahweh's self-declaration which provides the authority and must be pronounced by the human delegate," the question whether this declaration was originally linked with the divine utterances concerning the commands about idolatry and other ones (except the later amplifications of Exodus 20, 5. 6) in the third person, is justified. This "inconsistency . . . prompts the suspicion that the beginning of the decalogue is not in its original form".[19] The body of ethical precepts must have been linked later on with the self-declaration, the reference to the deliverance from Egypt, and the basic prohibition of idolatry based on some form of convenant by way of example (about which more below).

In the book of the covenant (Ex. 20, 22–23. 33), too, the negative commands of Exodus 22, 20ff. have been given the form of divine utterances later on;[20] when the self-declaration is lacking, Exodus

[18] Cf. W. Zimmerli, "Ich bin Jahwe," in *Alt-Festschrift* (1953), pp. 179–209; K. Elliger, "Ich bin der Herr-Euer Gott," in *Heim-Festschrift* (1954), pp. 9–34.

[19] M. Noth, *Das zweite Buch Mose. Das Alte Test. Deutsch* (1959), p. 130.

[20] Cf. E. Gerstenberger, *op. cit.*, p. 56: ". . . (it) is sufficiently clear that the series of negative commands of Ex. 22, 20a. 21. 27. 23, 1–3, 6–9 have been inserted in Yahweh's discourse or framed by it in the course of a later compilation or by some reviser."

22, 20ff. goes back to before the case-law section in order to find the divine formula in Exodus 20, 22ff. In the same way the divine "I" of Exodus 34, 12ff. 18. 19. 20. 24. 25, alternates with the divine "He" of Exodus 34, 10. 14. 23. 24. 26. A decision about the original connection between the "liturgical decalogue" with a divine utterance is made very difficult because of the question[21] whether it is possible to extract a decalogue and to see how it is related to Exodus 23, 14–19. There are similar commands (Ex. 13, 3. 7; Deut. 16, 3. 16) which have no divine "I". In the law on godliness we have in Leviticus 18 originally an ancient decalogue for the protection of the family in the wide sense, then a decalogue about the forbidden degrees of affinity and two skeleton laws; the latter two have the self-proclamation. The self-proclamation formulas and the first person suffixes of Leviticus 19 (except, perhaps, v. 12) are additions.[22]

In conclusion, for most statutory formulas we must reckon with a derived connection between these formulas and a divine utterance. It is then also possible that the liturgical background and the divine authority of these formulas arose only in a later phase of theological thought where the ethical, moral, social and cultural commands where put under the authority and protection of Yahweh and his covenant.

2. The Decalogue, Statutory Law and the Convenant of Sinai

Within the large pericope about Sinai (Ex. 19, 1—Num. 10, 10) we may roughly separate the Yahwist (J) source (Ex. 19–24; 32–34) from the Priestly (P) source (Ex. 25–31; 35—Num. 10, 10).[23]

[21] Cf. J. J. Stamm, "Dreiszig Jahre Dekologforschung," in *Theologische Rundschau* (1961), pp. 220–3; together with this, Kl. Baltzer, *Das Bundesformular* (Neukirchen, 1960), pp. 48f.; W. Beyerlin, *Herkunft und Geschichte der ältesten Sinaitradition* (1961), pp. 30f. and 90ff. Recently H. Kosmala ("The so-called ritual decalogue" in *An. Swed. Theol. Inst.* I, 1962, pp. 31–61) has compiled an ancient calendar of feasts (vv. 18–24) and four other instructions about the feast of the Passover from Ex. 34, 14–26.

[22] Cf. K. Elliger, "Das Gesetz Leviticus 18," in *Zeitschrift für die alttestamentische Wissenschaft* 67 (1955), pp. 1–25. Similarly, R. Kilian, *op. cit.* (Diss. Masch.), pp. 21ff. for Lev. 18 and 36ff. for Lev. 19; see also E. Gerstenberger, *op. cit.*, p. 58.

[23] Cf. G. von Rad, "Das formgeschtliche Problem des Hexateuch," in *Beitr. Wiss. Alt. u. N. Test.* IV (1938), p. 2b, also in *Gesammelte Studien zum*

Within the Yahwist pericope the decalogue (Ex. 20, 1–17) forms a definite unity, which has its place between Exodus 20, 18–21 and 24, 1–15 according to the best literary and historical criticism. Exodus 20, 1 links the decalogue in some original form with the Elohist section, 24, 3–8, and inserts it in that tradition.[24] Even if it is not possible to show an original literary connection with the Sinai account, a certain correspondence in the form is found in the self-presentation of Yahweh, the introductory reference to the deliverance from Egypt and in the prohibition to worship alien gods and images.

The book of the covenant (Ex. 20, 22–23. 33) must probably also be considered as an independent law book, later inserted between the accounts of the theophany (19, 1–20. 21) and the conclusion of the covenant (24, 1–11). The worship regulations of Exodus 23, 13–19 (cf. Ex. 34, 14–26) seem to have originated in the tradition of the surrounding culture and to have been added later to the body of laws; the second supplement (Ex. 23, 20–33) has developed gradually and may be taken "as winding up the section on the law as happens in Deuteronomy 27ff. and Leviticus 26".[25]

In contrast with the decalogue of Exodus 20 and the book of the covenant of Exodus 20, 22–23. 33, the so-called liturgical decalogue of the Yahwist tradition (Ex. 34, 10–28) appears, with its mention of the covenant in verses 10 and 27 and its preoccupation with worship, as a "liturgical fragment (exhortation and regulation of the feasts), which, however, lack the other elements of the liturgy of the covenant, for whatever reason".[26] Baltzer[27] and others have sorted out the main elements of the draft of a covenant: the reference to the previously existing situation, declaration of the main principle, particular commands and conclusion. The archaic expression "to cut a covenant" (vv. 10 and 27) is interesting as it refers to the original rite of making a covenant by carving up a

---

A.T. (1958), pp. 9–86, here pp. 20ff.; M. Noth, *Überlieferungsgeschichte des Pentateuch* (1948), pp. 13ff. and elsewhere.

[24] For the question of the sources of the decalogue, see the various hypotheses listed by J. J. Stamm, *op. cit.*, pp. 218ff.

[25] W. Beyerlin, *op. cit.*, p. 9.

[26] E. Gerstenberger, *op. cit.*, p. 83.

[27] Baltzer, *op. cit.*, pp. 48ff.

sacrificial animal (cf. Gen. 15, 9f. and 17; Jer. 34, 18f.). The "ten words" (Ex. 34, 28), which can be isolated from the text (Ex. 34, 10–28), represent perhaps the deed of covenant according to the Yahwist tradition. With its anti-Canaanite slant it reflects perhaps "the danger of complete assimilation to the Canaanites and the need to secure the basic tenets of Yahweh's covenant and worship".[28]

Apart from the literary problem of the relation between the decalogue and the covenant, which cannot be solved, partly because of the complex situation of the Sinai pericope, there are two further problems. The first concerns the growth of the formulary of the covenant, the second deals with the historical development of a cult. These two problems are prominent in contemporary studies.

S. Mowinckel[29] places the decalogue in the worship connected with God's "accession to the throne" and the new year when, according to Psalms 81 and 50 and Deuteronomy 31, 10–13, liturgical prophets read out collections of laws; according to Psalms 15 and 24 the decalogues constitute the instructions before entering the temple and taking part in the worship. In Alt's view the decalogue and other statutory precepts are read out for the service of the tabernacles every seventh year, according to Deuteronomy 27 and 31, 10–31. In Deuteronomy von Rad distinguishes the following formal elements:[30]

1. historical presentation of the events of Sinai and exhortation: Deut. 1–11;
2. recitation of the law: Deut. 12–26, 15;
3. obligations of the covenant: Deut. 26, 16–19;
4. blessing and curse: Deut. 27ff.

---

[28] W. Beyerlin, *op. cit.*, pp. 101f. and 108. This author holds that the decalogue of Exodus 34 has been displaced by the anti-Canaanite laws of Exodus 34, 10–28. Cf. N. Lohfink, "Der Dekalog in der Sicht heutiger Bibelwissenschaft," in *Religionsunterricht an Höheren Schulen* 6 (1963), pp. 197–206, here p. 205, note 13: "There is much to suggest that the text of the covenant in Exodus 34 represents the original document in the strict sense of the word."

[29] *Le décalogue* (Paris, 1927); *idem*, "Zur Geschichte der Dekaloge," in *Zeitschrift für die alttestamentische Wissenschaft* 55 (1937), pp. 218–35.

[30] *Op. cit.*, pp. 34f.

In the same way he distinguishes the following elements in the Sinai pericope:

1. exhortation (Ex. 19, 4–6) and historical presentation of the events of Sinai (Ex. 19f.);
2. recitation of the law (decalogue and covenant book);
3. promise of blessing (Ex. 23, 20ff.);
4. conclusion of the covenant (Ex. 24).

He gives a similar analysis of Jos. 24.

New pointers were contained in the work of G. E. Mendenhall[31] who showed an affinity with contractual formulas in the Hittite treaties of the 14th and 13th centuries B.C., while further investigations were made by K. Baltzer[32] and D. J. McCarthy[33] in the formulary of the covenant in the Old Testament and the East.

3. *Analogies with the Covenant and the Decalogue in the Ancient East*

Among the ancient oriental covenants the so-called suzerainty treaties of the Hittites,[34] in which a vassal binds himself to the king under oath, show the following structure:

1. preamble (with name and title of the king);
2. historical introduction (referring to previous relations between the partners, and particularly to the favors bestowed by the king);
3. basic principle or statement of authority (with the basic demand for the partner's loyalty, prohibition of relations with foreign powers, the prohibition of hostilities, the duty to serve, etc.);
4. particular clauses (referring to boundaries, tribute, military assistance, etc.);
5. order to keep a copy of the treaty in the temple and to have it read out at regular intervals;

---

[31] *Law and Covenant in Israel and the Ancient Near East* (Pittsburgh, 1955).
[32] *Op. cit.*
[33] "Treaty and Covenant," in *Analecta Biblica* 21 (Rome, 1963).
[34] The table with the formal elements of all the Hittite treaties is given in McCarthy, *op. cit.*, p. 50.

6. call on the god as witness;

7. curse and blessing.

It is particularly instructive to compare the form of this treaty with that of the Sichem covenant[35] in Josue 24 and that of Deuteronomy. There is only a partial correspondence with the Sinai pericope and the sections in which it has been transmitted. It is doubtful whether the oldest traditions of the Pentateuch have any connection with this kind of suzerainty treaty or with Josue 24.[36] Even when in some sections of the Sinai pericope isolated elements show an affinity with the Hittite formula, the literary context, the tone and the main point are different. In Exodus 19–24 the main accent falls on the power and glory of Yahweh. In Exodus 24, 1–2 and 9–11 the center of the covenant is a meal, and this ritual meal of the covenant has no connection with the treaties. It is also curious that the curse-and-blessing formulas are absent from the Yahwist tradition.

Alt's contention that genuine Isralite law in the Old Testament is unique and exclusive is refuted by numerous statutory formulas in the Hittite treaties.[37] The form of statutory law, therefore, is no longer an argument for the authentic Israelite character of the decalogue and the negative commands.

On the other hand, the clauses of the treaties and those of the decalogue or the covenant have little in common. Gerstenberger[38] has given sound reasons why we cannot identify the negative commands of the treaties with those of the Old Testament. The treaty conditions are political in form and contents, and envisage a concrete person, often by name. In the Old Testament the serialization of negative commands is typical, and this occurs mostly in the treaties when a breach of contract is visualized. Heinemann[39] and

---

[35] See particularly the studies of Baltzer and McCarthy, and also J. L'Hour, "L'Alliance de Sichem," in *Revue Biblique* 69 (1962), pp. 5–36, 161–84, 350–68, and G. Schmitt, *Der Landtag von Sichem* (Stuttgart, 1964).

[36] See particularly the explanations given by McCarthy, *op. cit.*, pp. 152ff.

[37] For the list, see McCarthy, *op. cit.*, p. 49.

[38] *Op. cit.*, pp. 87–91.

[39] *Untersuchungen zum apodiktischen Recht*, Diss. Masch. (Hamburg, 1958), only known to me through Stamm and Gerstenberger.

von Reventlow[40] try to explain these differences by referring to a difference in the situation; von Reventlow tried to derive a "common original form" from the "liturgical covenant form of Israel" and the "profane and political treaty form of the Hittite kingdom", but his arguments are not convincing.

III

DECALOGUE, STATUTORY LAW AND "WISDOM"

1. *The Statute—Exhortation and Warning*

In the wisdom literature of the Old Testament, as in that of the ancient East, we may distinguish between impersonal, objective sentences and personal, direct exhortations and warnings.[41] Instructions of the latter kind may be found in Proverbs 1–9; 22, 17–24. 22. They do not, however, show any relevant parallels[42] in form or content with statutory statements.[43]

By way of example I give the following:

Prov. 22, 22	Amenemope c.2	Lev. 19, 13
Prov. 22, 28	Amenomope c.6	Deut. 19, 14
Prov. 23, 10	Amenomope c.6	Ex. 22, 21.

W. Kornfeld[44] rejects the striking parallelism because Proverbs have a different character: "they are not addressed to a real person, but to a fictitious one, called 'my son'." When he says that they are maxims that do not claim to be "laws", then this applies also largely to the early negative commands. His mistake lies in the fact that he judges the statutory positive and negative commands from the final redaction of Yahweh's speech, and starts from the later insertion of the sentences in the tradition of Sinai and Horeb. The warnings and exhortations of both the wisdom literature and the

[40] *Op. cit.* pp. 276f.
[41] Cf. W. Baumgartner, in *Zeitschrift für die alttestamentische Wissenschaft* 34 (1914), pp. 161–98; H. Gese, *Lehre und Wirklichkeit in der alt. Weisheit* (Tübingen, 1958) pp. 51f.; E. J. Gordon, *Sumerian Proverbs* (Philadelphia, 1959), pp. 1ff.; J. J. van Dijk, *La sagesse Suméro-Accadienne* (Leiden, 1953); Gerstenberger, *op. cit.*, pp. 100ff.
[42] Cf. Gerstenberger, *loc. cit.*
[43] *Idem, op. cit.*, p. 169, n. 131.
[44] *Studien zum Heiligkeitsgesetz* (Vienna, 1952), pp. 59f.

statutes were adapted to the actual stage of instruction; father-son, head of the family—member of the family, head of the tribe—free citizen, teacher (instructor)—pupil, and so on. As these exhortations were included in the divine speech and the events of Sinai, the authority changed accordingly and at the same time the obligation became as absolute as the divine authority.

2. Analogies with Egyptian Wisdom Literature

In Egypt this literature is transmitted in proverbs or sayings composed of brief lines of about equal length in order "to smooth the path of the realization of the divine order which, in essence, is fully removed from all human influences . . ." [45] There is but one order, one truth, which is valid in the human domain as in the divine. Any offense against this true order is avenged by misfortune in life on this earth. This way of life is traced in numerous rules and sayings. "All the teaching applies to all men insofar as they belong to the social group to which they are addressed".[46] In the moral maxims[47] of the time of Ramses II we find two series of ten; every maxim begins with "do not," "thou shalt not":

Prepare not thyself on this day for tomorrow ere it be come; is not (?) yesterday like today upon the hands of God?

Mock (?) not at an old man or woman when they are decrepit; beware lest (Rt. 3) they . . . thee before thou growest old.

Recognize not one (as) thy mother, who is not; behold it will be heard by . . .

Straighten not what is crooked that thou mayest gain love; estimate (?) every man according to his character like a member of himself.

Boast not of thy strength whilst thou art a stripling; tomorrow will be found for thee as bitter berries upon the lip.

Take not a large bite of the king's property; beware lest . . . swallow thee.

[45] H. Brunner, "Die Weisheitsliteratur," in *Handbuch der Orientalistik* I, 2 (Literature 1952), pp. 90–110, especially p. 93.

[46] Brunner, *op. cit.*, p. 95.

[47] A. Gardiner, "A New Moralizing Text," in *Herm. Junker-Festschrift, Wiener Zeit. f. die Kunde des Morgenl.* 54 (1957), pp. 44f.

. . . the king's house at the door . . .

(*Two* (?) *lines lost*)

Spare not thy limbs whilst thou art a stripling; food comes through the hands and provisions through the feet.

Boast not of things which are not thine; another time (thou wilt be?) stealing or transgressing commands.

Denounce not a crime which is becoming (?) small; a mast has been seen lying as a foot.

Denounce not a small crime, beware lest it grow; a ship's carpenter can (?) raise it up like a mast.

Meditate not plans for the morrow; it has not yet come today until tomorrow comes.

Be not ignorant about thy neighbours in the days of their troubles, so that they turn for thee around thee in (thy) moment.

Make not thy marriage without thy neighbours, so that they may turn to thee (with) mourning on the day of burial.

Boast not of grain at time of ploughing, that it (?) may be seen on the threshing-floor.

Be not stubborn in fighting with thy neighbours; thy allies (?) . . . (Vs. 10) vigilant (?), know(?) . . .

As a further illustration I give a few sayings from the teaching of Amenemope:[48]

Do not remove the boundary stone from the boundaries of the field and do not shift the course of the measuring string; do not covet a yard of field and do not pull up the boundary of a widow.

Do not covet the goods of a small man, and do not hunger for his bread.

Do not falsely fix the hand-scales, do not use false weights, do not reduce the parts of the corn-measure.

Bring no man to misfortune by means of justice and do not twist justice.

Do not laugh at a blind man and do not mock at a dwarf, do not bring the lame one's purpose to disgrace.

[48] Transl. by Fr. W. von Bissing, *Altägyptische Lebensweisheit* (Zürich, 1955), pp. 82, 84, 86, 87, 89.

The so-called negative confession, a statement made by the dead
person before the tribunal of the other world, "expresses an ethical
order embracing the whole extent of human obligations, and works
out to a very fine shade the various offenses against the neighbor,
which constitute the main concern of ethics".[49] A good example
may be found in the introduction to chapter 125 of the so-called
Book of the Dead:

I have not made ill. I have not caused tears.
I have not killed. I have not given the order to kill.
I have made no man suffer.
I have not diminished the food in the temples.
I have not damaged the sacrificial loaves of the gods.
I have not stolen the sacrificial bread of the dead.
I have not had unlawful intercourse.
I have not indulged in unnatural vice . . .[50]

According to the Stele of Beki[51] and linking up with chapter 125,
just quoted, the dead person says that "he has let himself be guided
by the laws (hp'w) of the hall of the two truths", which means that
the sentences of the so-called negative confession have the value
of commandments in ordinary life. "I have not killed" is the equivalent of the commandment "Thou shalt not kill". It is quite possible that Moses knew of these moral maxims, which show an ethical
affinity with the decalogue, from his life in Egypt.[52] In these texts
man is not so much concerned with the practice of magic, or with
asserting himself and forcing the gods as O. Schilling thinks, but
rather shows a genuine ethical concern with the human order, as
one can see in the idealized biographies of the Middle Kingdom
and the wisdom literature. The idealized biography "tries to ex-

[49] J. Spiegel, "Die Idee vom Totengericht in der ägyptischen Religion,"
in *Leipziger Ägyptol. Studien* (1935), p. 59.
[50] Transl. by Spiegel, *op. cit.*, p. 57; cf. H. Gressmann, *Altorient. Texte z.
Texte der A.T.* 2 (Berlin, 1926), pp. 10f.
[51] Spiegel, *op. cit.*, p. 74.
[52] Similarly, but without the reference to the "laws of the hall of both
truths", Cazelles, "Loi israélite," in *Dict. Bibl. Supp.* V (1952), c. 515: "But
Moses, the former scribe . . . turned a protestation of innocence after death
into a command for the living."

press the ideal type and the ethical order of a particular sphere of life (of a high official, perhaps, or a courtier)", but the negative confession at the judgment of the dead "develops the ideal of justice and the ethical order for all men and contains no reference to any particular class".[53]

King Haremheb's decree[54] contains precepts and maxims suitable for judges, for instance, IV, line 14:

Do not associate with other people.
Do not accept bribes from others.

The ceremonial investitute of the vizir during the 18th dynasty numbered among its standing requirements[55] his moral obligations and the King's wish that these obligations should be fulfilled. Examples of these are:

Do not pass by a petitioner,
without considering his request.

Do not turn in anger against a man with injustice,
but be angry with that which requires anger.

In Sumerian and Babylonian-Assurian literature, too, there are, apart from the proverbs and sayings, monitory and exhortatory maxims formulated in the negative and in the second person singular.

After the deliverance from Egypt and the regular renewal of the covenant of Sinai-Horeb man can only express his communal and individual ethos "before Yahweh". Israel knows that "such a thing is not done in Israel" (Gen. 34, 7; 2 Sam. 13, 12). Morals, justice and law are placed under the will of Yahweh by the expression "I am Yahweh" which lends them authority and sanction. The

[53] Spiegel, *op. cit.*, p. 59.
[54] Cf. K. Pflüger, "The Edict of King Haremheb," in *Journal of Near Eastern Studies* 5 (1946), pp. 260–76; W. Helck, "Das Dekret des Königs Haremheb," in *Zeitschr. f. Ägypt. Spr. u. Altertumskunde* 80 (1955), pp. 109–36; see also H. Cazelles, "Moïse devant l'Histoire," in *Moïse l'homme de l'Alliance* (1955), p. 16; R. Kilian, "Apodiktisches und kasuistisches Recht, etc.", *loc. cit.*, pp. 199ff.
[55] K. Sethe, "Die Einsetzung des Veziers unter der 18. Dynastie. Inschrift im Grabe des Rech-mi-re su Schch abd el Gurna," in *Untersuchungen zur Geschichte und Altertumskunde Ägyptens* V, 2 (1909), p. 54.

community envisaged by the decalogue and other moral maxims is from then on "not any profane community, such as a State, still less the human society, but the community of Yahweh".[56] And just as Israel's faith marks the life and history of the community, so does the history of Israel mark its faith and ethics. The decalogue is therefore "anything but a summary of natural law; it is rather the proclamation of the law of the covenant . . . This law flows from God's majesty and grace, which seeks out man".[57] The proclamation of the decalogue calls Israel to obedience, and this duty of obedience contains the framework that marks off the minimum moral and religious possibilities within the community of the covenant. Even the beginnings of international ethics and law, as expressed, for instance, in the international poem of Amos 1–2, start from the will and majesty of Yahweh.

IV

FROM INSTRUCTION TO DIVINE COMMAND

Gerstenberger deserves credit for having made the order of the family the starting-point for statutory law, instead of worship or some feast. "The ethos of the family, revealed in negative commands, was watched over, transmitted and developed by those that had authority in the community, *i.e.*, the eldest among the blood relations".[58] It is therefore natural that family morals alternate with ordinary rules of daily life. The moral code developed naturally with the expansion of social relationships; the code had to be adapted to the changing situation in order to protect this situation as it developed.

The decisive and real beginning of Israel's salvation history is its deliverance from Egypt and the conclusion of the covenant on Sinai. These events marked the Israelites' faith in such a way that they saw their whole life and their society as linked with the One who saved them and made a covenant with them. Yahweh himself

[56] G. von Rad, *Theologie des Alten Testaments* I (Munich, 1957), pp. 196f.
[57] F. Horst, *Gottes Recht* (Munich, 1961), p. 257.
[58] *Op. cit.*, p. 114.

replaces the father and the elder of the tribe and it is his authority that creates the obligation. In a sociological analysis of the decalogue W. Schöllgen[59] came to the conclusion that "we can consider the ten commandments both as ethos and as ethics. They represent an ethos insofar as Yahweh's law creates a definite, concrete, historical nationhood . . . each of the ten commandments covers and protects a piece of life before the State exists . . . and only one will is paramount in this order, the will of God". God's self-revelation address takes over the basic moral maxims and negative rules for the guidance of the community. It pronounces the order of the covenant as the will of God and the people as the people of the covenant. Yahweh's self-presentation, in which he lays claim to being the deliverer from Egypt, reinforces the connection between saving will, saving deed and the demands of the covenant. There is no reason why Moses[60] should not have developed the style of maxims, rules and negative confessions, common in Egypt, and the half nomadic tribal rules (statutory or of the "wisdom" kind) in order to set up a "basic law for the newly created community of Yahweh",[61] and place it under the will of God.

As the community of the covenant developed its worship and ethos, Yahweh's will, expressed in the decalogue, would be drawn into the ceremonial cult and feasts (cf. Deut. 31, 10–13). Series of offenses to be cursed or punished by death or by exile would be composed for special occasions and in harmony with the decalogue:[62]

	Decalogue	Death Penalty	Curses
Worship of alien gods	Ex. 20, 3	Ex. 22, 19	
Worship of images	Ex. 20, 4		Deut. 27, 15
Misuse of Yahweh's name	Ex. 20, 7	Lev. 24, 16	
Sabbath	Ex. 20, 8	Ex. 31, 15	

[59] *Der Dekalog unter soziologischem Gesichtspunkt. Aktuelle Moral Probleme* (Düsseldorf, 1955), pp. 44–55.

[60] For the age of the decalogue, see the various hypotheses in Stamm, *op. cit.*, pp. 226–34.

[61] E. Sellin, *Einleitung in das A. T.*, 8th ed. (1949), p. 25.

[62] Alt, *op. cit.*, p. 320.

Cursing one's parents	Ex. 20, 12	Ex. 21, 17	Deut. 27, 16
Murder	Ex. 20, 13	Ex. 21, 12	Deut. 27, 24
Adultery	Ex. 20, 14	Lev. 20, 10	
Theft	Ex. 20, 15	Ex. 21, 16	

The passage of Deuteronomy 27, 11ff., which dates certainly from before Deuteronomy, still clearly shows the liturgy of the renewal of the covenant: the twelve tribes are divided into two groups, one on Mount Ebal and one on Mount Gerizim; there they respond antiphonally with curse or blessing or confirm with an "amen" the dodecalogue of crimes to be cursed. Yahweh's will applies also to "secret" actions (vv. 15 and 24): "Israel makes itself the instrument for the fulfillment of God's will by introducing this will into all the ramifications of life."[63]

A very early "case-law" elaboration of the decalogue may be found in the list of crimes to be cursed in Deuteronomy 13, 2—24, 7.[64]

Insofar as Deuteronomy adapts the decalogue to the present through exhortation and commentary, it makes an important contribution to the formation of a covenant ethos. According to N. Lohfink,[65] Deuteronomy 6, 12–16 provides "the main prop for the framework built round the great commandment, a commentary on the principal commandment of the decalogue". In Deuteronomy "the fulfillment of the principal commandment and the observance of all commandments" are not related "as a part to a whole . . . but as two aspects of one and the same thing".[66]

The law of sanctification shows how old regulations for the protection of family and kindred are developed in the direction of salvation history, theology and pastoral care. For instance, Leviticus 18 contains a decalogue dealing with the sexual protection of blood-relations in a half nomadic family in the wider sense: "You

[63] G. von Rad, *Das fünfte Buch Mose*, p. 121.
[64] Cf. J. L'Hour, "Une législation criminelle dans Deutéronome," in *Bibl.* 44 (1963), pp. 1–28.
[65] "Das Hauptgebot," in *Analecta Biblica* 20 (Rome, 1963), p. 154.
[66] *Op. cit.*, p. 159. See also p. 158: "To observe all the commandments and to fulfill the concrete demand of the main command as understood at the time is the same thing."

shall not uncover the nakedness of . . ." At a further stage this becomes a dodecalogue of forbidden affinity relations (v. 7–16 and 13, 17 as well as the additions in 9 and 10). Lastly, it is fitted into the perspective of salvation history (2b–4. 24. 30; 5, 25–29) "by situating it in the period after the exodus from Egypt but before the expulsion of the Canaanites" and "thus the law of Leviticus 18 becomes part of the historical presentation of the events of Sinai according to the Priestly tradition of the Pentateuch".[67] Reward and punishment, promise and threat help to inculcate the commandments. This constant expansion of the decalogue through the introduction of amendments and its insertion into the Sinai traditions finally led to the formation of the all-embracing Torah in the new setup of the post-exilic community. Its observance is stressed in Deuteronomy 30, 19–20: "Choose life, then, that you and your descendants may live, by loving the Lord, your God, heeding his voice, and holding fast to him. For that will mean life for you, a long life for you to live . . ."

Psalms 11, 19b and 119 show a culminating point in the theological appreciation of the Torah: in the Torah the Psalmist meets his God of the covenant and experiences in the law the self-witness of Yahweh, which brings with it comfort, wisdom, joy, strength to live, justice and peace. The epithets of the Torah—perfection, trustworthiness, uprightness, integrity, truth, worthiness and sweetness—show an almost sacramental approach. According to Jeremiah 31, 34, joy in being instructed by God's law is a sign of the eschatological existence of the just man.[68]

[67] K. Elliger, "Das Gesetz Leviticus 18," in *Zeitschrift für die alttestamentische Wissenschaft* 67 (1955), pp. 1–25; compare with this the research done by Kilian and von Reventlow and others on the law of sanctity; see Elliger, *op. cit.*, p. 20.

[68] Cf. H. J. Kraus, "Freude an Gottes Gesetz," in *Evangelische Theologie* (1950/51), pp. 337–51; G. J. Botterweck, in *Theologische Quartalschrift* 138 (1958), pp. 129–51; A. Deissler, "Psalm 119 und seine Theologie," in *Münchener theologische Studien* I (1955), p. 11.

V

FULFILLMENT IN CHRIST

When speaking to a scribe Jesus himself designated the double command of love of God and love of neighbor (Mk. 12, 28–34; Matt. 22, 34–40; Luke 10, 25–29) as the norm: "On these two commandments depend the whole Law and the Prophets" (Matt. 22, 40). This absolute double commandment of love corresponds to Deuteronomy 6, 4f. and Leviticus 19, 18. Insofar as the commandments and laws of the Old Testament correspond to this double norm, they remain binding. According to Matt. 5, 17, Jesus does not represent the abolition of the law and the prophets but their fulfillment. Since God's dominion is inaugurated in Jesus, he is also the authoritative proclaimer and interpreter of God's will. Paul's Gospel of radical freedom from the law is rooted in his faith in Christ and in his soteriology. In the Gospel of our salvation by God through the death of Jesus, the Gospel of the absolute penetration of human activity by grace, Christ is ultimately the end of the law (Rom. 10, 4).[69]

[69] Cf. P. Glaser, "Gesetz, III N.T." in *Lexicon für Theologie und Kirche* II, 2 (1958), pp. 820–2, and particularly R. Schnackenburg, "Biblische Ethik II, N. T.," in *Lexicon für Theologie und Kirche* II, 2nd ed. (1958), pp. 429–33, and the bibliography given there.

René Coste / *Toulouse, France*

Pacifism and Legitimate Defense

This article does not aim at controversy but rather at establishing a dialogue between two contradictory attitudes toward war: absolute pacifism and legitimate collective defense. Total pacifists deny the legitimacy of any war, even when it is a case of resisting outright aggression. The more consistent pacifist refuses to allow any deliberate shedding of blood, any use of violence, even to prevent a crime where he is an eye-witness.

On the other hand, those who hold the principle of legitimate collective defense maintain that this is a matter of an inherent right of man. For them, only violence can stop the spread of violence, whether at the individual or the collective level. Theoretically at least, they do not claim that *any* war is justified except a war of defense against an aggressor. The total pacifists reproach the advocates of collective defense for behaving like barbarians and perpetuating the law of the jungle. The latter reply that the total pacifist is lucky that others are ready to dirty their hands in protecting his peace.

Accusations of being war-minded or unrealistic and even cowardly are bandied about. Often a certain amount of contempt creeps in. The one who feels he has a clear conscience considers that the other indulges in immoral compromise, and the realist considers that the pacifist suffers from dangerous illusions. The dialogue is difficult and often impossible; both sides are incapable of listening carefully to the other's argument. One may notice this at any judicial hearing for conscientious objectors: one gets the painful impression that there is an abyss dividing the judges and the young man who appears before them honest though they all are.

Would it not be a good thing if both parties were to exchange some ideas in a genuine attempt to understand each other? Would this not at least force both sides to clarify their own thought in order the better to answer the other's objections? Perhaps they would then find some common ground, or, if one prefers, some *via media* along which they could walk together. In this article I shall try to chart a *via media*, dividing the argument into three stages: (I) the characteristics of total pacifism; (II) a critical evaluation of total pacifism, and (III) relative pacifism, or how to reconcile two extremes.

I

CHARACTERISTICS OF TOTAL PACIFISM

Although pacifism knows a whole spectrum of very subtle shades that make a complete classification almost impossible, we may bypass the differences of vocabulary and even of definite motivation, and distinguish four main categories: (1) sentimental pacifism, (2) rational pacifism, (3) total nonviolence of the Eastern or humanist type, and (4) total pacifism inspired by Christianity. I shall describe their essential features as they present themselves today.

1. *Sentimental Pacifism*

Sentimental pacifism sprang from the horrors of war. The smoking ruins of vast cities, the savagery of the fighting, the agony of the dying and the permanent scars of mutilated bodies created a pacifist reaction in many men and women who witnessed that misery. Why this wastage of material riches and human lives? If only we could be sure that our sacrifice would bring about a lasting peace. Look at those who fought in World War I. They faced the mud and the long watches in the trenches hoping that the hell into which they had been plunged would vanish forever. Twenty years later their sons, and sometimes they themselves, were forced to start all over again.

Who can be sure that this sinister game will not soon begin again, though infinitely worse because of the new weapons that man has invented? For these men and women the ideals of justice are but pale, abstract notions. Often they themselves would be ready to face death, but the death of their dear ones is intolerable to them. Some would not go so far as to sacrifice themselves. For them, individual existence ends in the grave, and physical life is therefore the supreme good. When one mentions the slavery to which a totalitarian State can reduce the majority of its citizens, they answer with the French expression: better a live dog than a dead lion. According to them, peace must be preserved at all costs whatever the consequences for spiritual values.

2. *Rational Pacifism*

Rational pacifism is different. It, too, was a reaction against the horrors of war, but it goes beyond sentiment and faces the problem of justice. The destruction of material goods, suffering and even death could be accepted if they had a meaning for justice. But that is precisely what seems impossible to the rational pacifist. Victory is not necessarily the triumph of might and the denial of right, since might by itself does not in any way confer any right. If a belligerent party happens to have backed a just cause and is fortunate enough to see it triumph, is that not sheer accident? In one way or another, it simply means that it has proved his military superiority. Moreever, both sides claim the right to legitimate defense, often in good faith. If necessary, propaganda can sow confusion, at least among those who fight on his side. The dictatorial peace of Versailles and the cowardice or lack of intelligence, for instance, are partly responsible for the aggressive policies of the Third Reich. However one looks at it, military battle cannot decide the justice and value of a cause.

When one passes from the question of objectives to that of the means, the contradiction is equally shocking. What can one think, from the moral point of view, of a process that only achieves its end by killing vast numbers of innocent people: soldiers forced to fight in a battle that they did not choose, and for which not they, but their leaders are responsible; women, the aged, children, all the victims of the bombing of cities? Do not weapons of mass destruction strike combatants and noncombatants alike? Is it not either absurd or hypocritical to want to humanize hostilities when one knows perfectly well that success can only be brought about by violence? So the rational pacifist concludes that war is radically irrational and unjust, and in no case is it possible to take part in it.

These two types of pacifism refuse to admit that collective defense can be legitimate, the first one only implicitly because of the practical conditions of warfare. But neither of these is opposed to individual defense. If attacked by a murderer, neither would hesitate to use violence or even, if necessary, to kill in order to save his own life. And neither is usually opposed to capital punishment for criminals. This is why, particularly in the first case, one cannot really speak of total pacifism. But this description *does* apply to the third and fourth categories.

3. *Eastern Total Pacifism*

Outside biblical thought, the oldest known teachings of total nonviolence are found in India. It is an essential feature of Buddhist morality, but it is older than that. All deliberate shedding of animal or human blood, all physical or moral violence are formally forbidden. The believer must be vegetarian, even if such a diet causes extreme practical difficulties (some may remember the moving confessions of Gandhi on this point in his autobiography). Violent means must be rejected, even to save one's life from a killer. At the most, one is allowed to flee in order to escape. The man who has killed all violence in himself shows the greater courage. He faces his killer in order that his gentleness may provoke a similar gentleness in the attacker who may have been waiting for someone to show him the way to overcome his hatred and other vices from which he may suffer.

This attitude seems to have its roots in the attitude of detachment toward present existence and in the acceptance of grief, two dispositions which are both embodied in a special philosophy. Whatever the theoretical basis, in many souls this attitude has flowered into an admirable compassion and genuine love. It has passed relatively recently from the East to the West where it linked up with the specifically Christian tradition. Those in the West who subscribe to the tradition of the East usually also claim to belong to the Christian tradition in the West, and find it often difficult to say what in their attitude derives from one source and what from the other. Nonviolence can indeed exist without faith in God. It is then simply the recognition (but how exacting!) of the principle that man, being a creature of intelligence and love, must act according to the demands of intelligence and love. One could describe this attitude as humanistic. Even though the believer must regret that this humanism does not accept the faith in a personal God, he will regard it with respect wherever he meets it.

4. *Christian Total Pacifism*

Christian total pacifism comes very close to the kind of pacifism just mentioned, but its source lies in the heart of the living God: the universal love of Jesus of Nazareth who revealed to us the infinite love of the Father, the Son and the Spirit. It takes the Sermon on the Mount seriously:

"You have heard that it was said, 'An eye for an eye', and, 'A tooth for a tooth'. But I say to you not to resist the evildoer; on the contrary, if someone strike thee on the right cheek, turn to him the other also. . . . You have heard that it was said, 'Thou shalt love thy neighbor and shalt hate thy enemy'. But I say to you, love your enemies, do good to those who hate you, and pray for those who persecute and calumniate you . . . For if you love those that love you, what reward shall you have? Do not even the publicans do that? . . . You therefore are to be perfect, even as your heavenly Father is perfect" (Matt. 5, 38–48).

Does this not make it clear that in these words our Lord rejected the principle of individual and, *a fortiori*, collective, legitimate defense at least where Christians are concerned? Does not the very clearness of Christ's words impose the rejection of all violent means under any circumstances, even if this leads to our death? Has he not himself set the example in the garden of Gethsemane? Is this not the way the martyrs understood him throughout the history of the Church? Would it not be blasphemous to try to reconcile war with evangelical love? According to this reasoning, then, every Christian should be a total pacifist.

II

CRITICAL EVALUATION OF TOTAL PACIFISM

This description of the essential features of total pacifism shows at once how wrong are those who look on it with disdain. Even if, as in my own case, we cannot wholly agree with it, it clearly contains a message that modern man cannot ignore, particularly if he wishes to live according to the Gospel, and this holds especially for rational pacifism, Eastern total pacifism and Christian total pacifism. I hope my criticism will show the respect it deserves. The clearest and most objective way of proceeding is to draw up a balance of the positive and negative elements contained in all four categories of total pacifism.

We can admit without hesitation that the positive contribution of total pacifism is considerable. This can be expressed in a few words in each case: sentimental pacifism shows a sane reaction; rational pacifism shows up the essential irrationality of war; Eastern total pacifism is the result of conduct worthy of man; and Christian total pacifism points up the demands of evangelical love.

Sentimental pacifism itself is not wholly negative in spite of the grave objections it provokes. It shows a sane reaction, at least in part; it stresses the value of all human life. It is normal that man should wish to preserve his life on this earth and that of those dear to him. It is normal that he should be indignant at the sight of the massacres of both World Wars. Life is a gift of God, which human society has a duty to protect and not to injure. This sensitiveness is better than the indifference with which politicians and strategists gamble away millions or even hundreds of millions of lives as if they were mere abstract figures in a mathematical calculation. Popular opinion is right in protesting against such inhuman schemes.

Rational pacifism shows up the essential irrationality of war. It is true that the immediate triumph of war lies only with the stronger. It is true that war is blind and hurts the innocent as much as the guilty. It is true that both sides claim legitimate defense. It is true that weapons of mass destruction make the conflict more and more inhuman. War cannot be taken as a normal political weapon. Only rarely does a State have the right to use collective armed resistance. Governments ought to have remembered those principles of natural law, particularly at the time when public law was formulated in Europe. The lightheartedness with which so many conflicts were provoked and accepted, as in 1914, even by men who claimed to be noble idealists, deserves severe condemnation.

Eastern or humanist nonviolence takes us a step further. Rational pacifism has a certain coldness about it, an element of impersonal justice. But here the rules are given inward life, are intensified and expanded by the warmth of the human person and of man, my brother. Since our being is spiritual and loving, the only means we can use are those of understanding and love. We must try in a peaceful manner to solve the conflicts that set us in opposition to each other, whether individually or collectively. With goodwill, understanding, imagination and courage, many seemingly insurmountable obstacles would disappear to the benefit of us all. Nor should we forget that "the other" is often better than we think because we are blinded by our prejudices and our pride. Trust provokes trust.

The Christian form of total pacifism forces us to shake off the dust and cinders that too often overlay the fiery words of the Gospel in our mind. It is an incontestable fact that Christ *did* preach nonviolence, both as a condition and a consequence of the universal love that he taught us. To pretend, as is sometimes done, that his directives are only meant to be applied to individual or ecclesial relationships is a supposition that is nowhere justified in the writings of the New Testament. Evangelical morality embraces the whole of human activity: only methods of application may differ according to the various levels at which it operates. The Christian, more than anyone else, is bound to use only peaceful means, both in his collective relationships and his individual ones. Otherwise, he is not faithful to the demands made by his master.

Must we therefore accept total pacifism, at least the kinds fully deserving the name (Eastern and Christian total pacificism)? This does not seem feasible because of serious objections that may be put to its lack of realism, except for sentimental pacifism, which is rather lacking in idealism.

Sentimental pacifism has been severely treated by Pius XII and Emmanuel Mounier, for example, and they are right. There is no doubt a healthy element in the wish to stay alive. But this wish must be given its proper place in the scale of values. If this wish becomes exclusive, or at least the primary wish, to the extent of despising or even denying spiritual values and leads to wrongful compromises, egotism or cowardice, then it becomes perverse and no longer deserves respect. One is not entitled to renounce the values that must inspire all human life worthy of that name for the sake of saving one's physical existence: *non propter vitam vitae perdere causas* (we must not save our life by losing the reasons for living). Man must learn to sacrifice himself.

But man must also be a realist. The very obligation to love others and to make society more fraternal imposes this realism because love aims at being effective. One can only master nature by accepting its laws and its concrete possibilities. So it is with human beings. If man were not a sinner and suffering from all kinds of disorderly elements, there would be no reason for legitimate defense because there would be no violence in human relationships. The theologians have pointed this out carefully: before original sin man was a harmonious being; the natural right to legitimate defense presupposes that man's break with God has introduced disorder. That is precisely our situation and not that of a humanity without sin and without disorder. Violence exists, and in many forms.

Let us look first at individual violence. Suppose I am attacked by a killer; am I bound to let him have his way, even though he has no claim on my life? Once he has succeeded in my case, will he not be encouraged to attack other innocent victims? The same thing holds at the collective level. A statesman sends an army to occupy a country and to impose a totalitarian regime on the population. Is one not entitled to try to prevent him from doing this? Should the world have remained inactive in face of Hitler's deeds? Must a violence that deprives millions of human beings of their basic rights not be opposed in the most effective way, short of means that themselves are contrary to natural law?

One has to accept the evidence: in many cases, individual or collective, only violence can stop the spread of violence, at least partially. If Gandhi had had to face a totalitarian government, he would no doubt have failed in his attempt to bring national independence to India. While wishing to make the world better, total pacifism would encourage the law of the jungle. That is why I cannot accept it as a general rule. Man must be changed first; this takes a long time and is a task that must constantly be begun all over again.

What is true for rational and Eastern total pacifism, holds also for Christian total pacifism. The love that the Gospel teaches must also be realistic because, like ordinary human love, it aims at being effective. Christ has indeed preached nonviolence (I have stressed that this must be taken seriously), but we must see this in the light of his teaching as a whole. One must then at least admit that it is not proven that he wanted Christians completely to abandon the natural right to self-defense. When I am attacked by a criminal, I may, out of love, refuse to defend myself. But when I see him threaten women, children and old people, am I entitled to abstain from violence because I am a Christian? Would I not be responsible then for the death of innocent people? The criminal has no right whatever to commit his crime.

This is how the early Church understood pacifism. That Church, which was so anxious to be faithful to directions given in the Gospel, clearly affirmed the right of legitimate defense, at least against common crime (*e.g.*, Rom. 13, 1–7). And later on, when the question of armed collective resistance arose in a concrete fashion, the Church of the first centuries usually gave the same answer in principle. St. Augustine, the great Doctor of love, thought it his duty clearly to assert this: Christians themselves are entitled to apply the right of legitimate collective defense against aggression in order to protect the city. In saying this, he and the theologians who followed him (almost unanimously) were convinced that in no way had they betrayed the Gospel.

III

RELATIVE PACIFISM, OR HOW TO RECONCILE TWO EXTREMES

These critical observations lead me to find a *via media*—the same one that St. Augustine followed—but adjusted to a new situation, and in essence pursuing the line traced by recent popes. It starts from the desire for peace as that of total pacifism, but it aims at being realistic. If the ground is uneven, then one cannot pretend it is otherwise.

The argument runs in three stages: the principle that makes it compulsory to settle international conflicts peacefully; the criteria for deciding whether collective resistance to aggression is legitimate; the rejection of a "mad" war and spiritual resistance. I shall add to this an important question that henceforth confronts the Christian conscience: total nonviolence as prophetic witness.

There are bound to be international conflicts, but they do not have to be solved by war. Political leaders can sit down around a table and sincerely try to find a basis of agreement by discussion (agreement by treaty) or let a third party decide (arbitrator or judge). Whatever the situation may be, they should try to behave like men, *i.e.*, beings capable of intelligence and love. As Pius XII said: "It is not by means of weapons, massacres and ruins that one can solve conflicts among men, but with reason, right, prudence and justice" (Encyclical "Laetamur admodum," Nov. 1, 1956, in *La Documentation Catholique* [1956], 1478–1479; *Discorsi e Radiomessaggi*, Vol. XVIII, p. 858). Theologians agree that the obligation to settle international disputes in a peaceful manner is demanded by natural law and explicitly confirmed by revelation.

The supposition that one party might not accept this principle, and might launch an armed attack, has so often been borne out by the facts that, unfortunately, it has to be considered. The realistic approach will then tell us that violence can only be stopped by violence. Objective criteria are necessary here to avoid self-deception. Traditional theology has laid down three conditions before armed collective resistance can be called justified: (1) injustice must be clearly established and proved to be extremely serious, thereby pointing to a situation where such defense is objectively and unquestionably legitimate; (2) the failure of every peaceful means; (3) the disastrous consequences of armed conflict must be less than the injustice that led to it (rule of the lesser evil). Most modern theologians maintain, with Pius XII, that these conditions may possibly be realized in two kinds of situations: an attack on the basic personal rights of a great number of human beings, and an attack on the existence (independence) of a State.

According to this third condition, it is also necessary to make sure that such collective resistance can bring about positive results at the general level of humanity. The right to legitimate defense, which alone can morally justify armed resistance, is not absolute. One cannot allow the kind of "mad" war that would cause excessive material and moral injury or that would offend the most elementary rules of human conduct. This is the doctrinal basis of the famous sentence in John XXIII's *Pacem in Terris*: "And for this reason it is hardly possible to imagine that in the atomic era war could be used as an instrument of justice" (n. 127).

It is indeed difficult to imagine that a nuclear war would not be, in fact, a "mad" war from the start, or at least would soon become "mad", because of the constant danger of going to extremes. Legitimate defense is not mutual self-destruction. In such a case, common sense demands the abandonment of armed collective resistance. Pius XII said in 1953: "To have recourse to violent warfare it is not enough to have to defend oneself against any kind of injustice. If the injury caused by warfare exceeds the injury suffered by tolerating the injustice done, one may be obliged to suffer that particular injustice" (Address given to the Sixteenth Congress of the International Bureau of Documentation on Military Medicine, October 19, 1953; *Discorsi e Radiomessaggi*, Vol. XV, p. 422).

The only resistance left, then, is spiritual resistance. This is far from being a surrender, and can lead to genuine victory. To quote a contemporary example, the effectiveness of this resistance is shown in the unswerving loyalty of so many of our brethren to their human and Christian ideals while they live under a totalitarian regime. It is true that this demands courage, a clear mind and a self-denial that is ready to face any sacrifice. But it is men of this calibre that we need so badly today. In the atomic era, this kind of resistance, which relies essentially on understanding and love, should be considered most seriously. Christians should be the first to examine its possibilities, without, of course, losing sight of the concrete reality in which we live.

To these clear principles of official Catholic doctrine, one must add the question of total nonviolence as prophetic witness. A number of modern theologians accept this factor. They agree that there may be people with an exceptional vocation, of a prophetic nature, whose mission it is to bear witness to universal love by the practice of total nonviolence, just as there are those who are called to the heroic practice of poverty, chastity and evangelical obedience.

In all these cases, the situation of such persons is only isolated in appearance. In the immediate environment their refusal to resort to violence in defense of victims of violence would, undoubtedly, not stop widespread movements (except, perhaps, in some extraordinary cases), but by slow and patient erosion, so to speak, they would wear out the hatred in man, or at least in some men. Their example would strengthen love on this earth. It would not be impossible to establish the authenticity of such vocations: disinterestedness, wish to serve, courage, spirit of sacrifice, habitual sound judgment, an intense spiritual life—all these factors would constitute genuine proof. Such an attitude would fall under the category of Christian total pacifism. The essential difference is that here this attitude is considered as an exceptional vocation and not as a general rule to be imposed on all Christians in a human reality that is marked by sin.

It is, therefore, possible to speak of a relative pacifism. It agrees with those who hold the principle of legitimate defense in accepting this principle. It agrees with total pacifism in that it stresses the principle of the obligatory settlement of international disputes by peaceful means. But given the sinful condition of mankind, it considers it necessary, or at least allowable on the basis of legitimate defense, to stop violence. This may not satisfy either camp, but should both parties not admit that the argument is coherent and that the objections to their attitude are valid? It reproaches the war-minded with not having enough faith in man and with too easily abandoning the ways of understanding and love. It reproaches the pacifists with a lack of realism and their failure to accept the concrete conditions for the building up of peace. The argument looks disconnected. But is not mankind itself disconnected? It is intensely involved in the duty to love all men. But does not Christ himself demand that we should love man as he is in his concrete situation? Like a house, peace is built up slowly, brick by brick. When an earthquake has destroyed all that has been built, the man of courage quite simply starts afresh.

EDITORIAL NOTE BY FRANZ BÖCKLE

René Coste's article is meant to invite discussion of this difficult and often fiercely controversial problem. Because of his objective presentation of the various attitudes, his contribution seems to provide a sound basis for further discussion. We would gladly examine, and possibly publish, any contributions with a sound theological foundation. The following points certainly need further clarification:

The Development of Pacifism in the History of Christianity

This should deal with pacifism during the reign of Constantine and the idea of peace in the City of God and lead on to the peace movements in the Middle Ages. (The Truce of God movement, the prohibition of Franciscan Tertiaries to carry arms, etc.)

The ABC War and Pacifism

The invention of atomic, bacteriological and chemical destructive weapons has turned the whole question of the conditions for a just war into a completely new problem. It has also opened a new phase in the discussion of whether modern war can be tolerated from the point of view of the Church. But if the Church did completely condemn any war of the ABC type—which is possible, and even necessary—this would still not necessarily mean that the Church subscribes to total pacifism. Two sets of problems remain:

1. The basic duty of the State to defend itself and the consequent duties of the individual. In this world, State and Church, the earthly kingdom and the kingdom of God do not coincide. The Church is Christ's kingdom; it stands under the sign of the cross and represents the mystery of redemption. The Church as a whole and all its members are called to imitate Christ, to renounce the violent defense of their rights, and to rely entirely on spiritual weapons. But what is valid for the Church and the individual Christian, is not necessarily applicable to the State as such. The State is not the Church, and in a sense it is more, namely, as the sum total of Christian citizens. It has, therefore, its own mission, its own purpose and its own functions. This difference in function shows particularly in the attitude toward injustice, which will never give up the right of the stronger in this sinful world.

There are good things that the State cannot abandon without

resistance; its office is to protect and defend law and order and the natural dignity and freedom of its citizens. This difference in aim can lead to serious conflict of conscience in those people who belong at the same time to the *Civitas Dei* and the *Civitas terrena.* The inner freedom of the Christian cannot be destroyed by any violence or servitude, however brutal. The only servitude is that of sin. Christian freedom does not coincide with civic freedom. It is possible that God uses outward infringements of our civic freedom in order to make us realize and appreciate the more the high value of our Christian freedom.

This, however, should not lead us to believe in a spiritualized Christianity detached from the world. The slogan of an imagined pure, realizable, unworldly Christianity would seem to us a dangerous illusion. True Christian freedom has the strength to express itself also outwardly in the recognition of human dignity and freedom. The free world owes, perhaps unconsciously and undeservedly, its freedom to the Christian concept of freedom. The Christian citizen will not lightly and weakly sacrifice these freedoms to a godless terrorism. Christian freedom must not be understood as being apolitical and asocial, but then it can keep away from the struggle for power without difficulty.

2. An overall appreciation of atomic war cannot include the demand that the "understanding", "Christian" side should renounce atomic weapons unilaterally. It is true that, if world peace rests only on the readiness to use atomic weapons if necessary, we live with the assumption that the ultimate catastrophe could happen. But if we still believe in a spark of human understanding beyond all human violence, we must attain disarmament with unconquerable patience and endurance and in very small stages. These questions put the Christian citizen on a steep and solitary ridge, threatened on both sides by a deadly abyss. To go this way demands decisions that are not easily set down and applied as a moral norm to all.

In a future volume of CONCILIUM it may be possible to deal with these problems more thoroughly.

PART II

BIBLIOGRAPHICAL SURVEY

Franz Böckle / *Bonn, W. Germany*

Birth Control

A Survey of German, French and Dutch
Literature on the Question of Birth Control

not for the refectory

I

THE BACKGROUND

1. There is no doubt that birth control has given rise to wide-spread and intense discussion. The most important reason for this is really that with the best will in the world the majority of our faithful find it impossible to live up to the demands of moral teaching about marriage as it stands today. Extensive inquiries addressed to Catholic doctors have confirmed again and again that in the regions covered by this survey, roughly 90 to 95 percent of fertile Catholic couples offend against the norms of this moral teaching more or less frequently. This is in itself no reason why the norms should be changed. We have no intention of letting statistics decide what is good and what is evil. But we must realize that these people are basically of goodwill; they wish to respect the Church and its message, and yet are driven to great distress in their very attempt to live up to this respect.

The well-known French periodical for married people, "L'an-neau d'Or", organized an inquiry among a large group of Catholic couples in view of the Council. The intention was to publish the replies in a special number, "Mariage et Concile". However,

AUTHOR'S NOTE: When an author and his work are more extensively discussed, the reference to the page of his work is given in parentheses in the body of the article.

instead of a full report on the findings there only appeared a brief statement[1] by the editors with the significant hint that it would be impossible to prevent this number from falling into the hands of people who might misunderstand the replies. It then goes on to say: "The moralists who have had to analyze the findings have been gravely disturbed by reading the replies of which there were about one thousand. What struck them most was that these families, so anxious to live their marriage in a Christian manner, to make their Christianity constantly more genuine, to give generously of their lives, and to take the Church's law seriously, are so profoundly perturbed by the problems created by birth control."

There follows a brief description of the physical and psychological distress of married people and attention is drawn to the perplexity besetting the priest. One harassed couple asks: "How can we take seriously this moral teaching on procreation when there is such a diversity of advice?" This question is asked by many today, and every priest with experience knows it.

2. What disturbs the moralist is not really the fact that a particular law is so frequently broken. He is much more worried by the conclusion that his norms are no longer adequate; that a considerable number of faithful and the clergy themselves think, insofar as birth control is concerned, that, the Church's teaching no longer corresponds to the needs of the time. Some historians object that this teaching contains too many Gnostic and Manichaean elements, or that what canon law says about the purpose of marriage can only be understood against the background of Ulpian's teaching on natural law and of the scholastic concept of genus and species. Here man is seen too much under his generic aspect (*in quantum est animal*) and too little under his specific human aspect (*in quantum est homo*). Much of this natural law, moreover, stems from a picture of nature that is no longer adequate or frankly out of date. Far too little attention is paid to man's historicity and the growth of knowledge about himself. The position of woman in the marital partnership has changed. Such

[1] *L'anneau d'Or*, 105–106 (Paris, May–August, 1962), p. 326.

questions and many others are now commonly posed.[2] They require a thorough examination of tradition by the theologians.

In this field Louis Janssens has drawn attention to the influence of Augustine's dualism on the teaching about marriage.[3] Augustine's view of the three "goods" (*bona*) of marriage has influenced Catholic tradition up to *Casti Connubii*. On the one hand, his pessimistic outlook on sexual desire and sexual joy forces him to look for a justification of these factors, and this he finds in the *bonum prolis* (children) and in the *bonum fidei* (faith). On the other hand, since he understands marital love as something purely spiritual, he finds it difficult to relate this to sexual life. He can only see sexual desire with its *malum concupiscentiae* (its evil lust) as an obstacle to conjugal love (p. 803). The more this sexual desire is repressed, the stronger marital love will be. Consequently, man possesses his wife "in holiness and honor" (1 Thess. 4, 4) insofar as he loves her spiritually and not carnally. Augustine would like to see all Christian marriages reach the state of complete continence.

This dualism of marital love and sexual love had a decisive influence in the following centuries. We find it in Hugh of St. Victor when he distinguishes two kinds of consent in marriage, the one relating to the spiritual unity of the partners, the other to their sexual bond. Spiritual unity is essential to marriage, the sexual bond is but a "conjoined" element, something "over and above". The great Scholastics have not accepted Hugh's views and only know of one consent. The marital bond includes the *right* to carnal union, but there is not yet an inner relationship between the two elements. This distinction between the essence (marital bond) and the effect (carnal union) is the basis of the marital doctrine of Albert the Great and Bonaventure. For them, marriage is essen-

[2] Cf. Leonhard M. Weber, *Mysterium magnum. Zur innerkirchlichen Diskussion um Ehe, Geschlecht und Jungfräulichkeit*, Quaestiones Disputatae (Freiburg, 1963), p. 9 and pp. 17ff. The same statements occur in a private report of German theologians.

[3] L. Janssens, "Morale conjugale et progestogènes," in *Ephemerides Theologicae Lovanienses* 39 (1963), pp. 787–826, esp. pp. 800–7.

tially a union of life and love between a man and a woman—seen by Bonaventure as a "union of souls". The "union of the bodies" does not belong to the essence but to the fullness of marriage. As soon as marriage is then considered in its fullness, that is, including the exercise of the right to each other's body, the *bonum prolis* immediately appears on the horizon so that the union in the flesh is still seen and judged in the tradition of Augustine.

Janssens thinks that the distinction made in the Roman Catechism between the two aspects of marriage goes back to this Augustinian and Franciscan tradition (p. 805). The dualism that Hugh of St. Victor created by his double consent, has therefore been overcome. The unity of marriage is seen in the unity of consent, but the sexual aspect is still very much a matter of choice between continence and the exercise of a right. I cannot understand why Anselm Günthör is so strongly opposed to Janssens' historical argument.[4] He writes: "The weakness of Janssens' historical survey and the consequent conclusions lies precisely in the briefness and lack of qualification of his argument" (p. 326). Janssens has devoted more than a third of his essay to this richly documented historical survey. A glance at the appropriate volumes of Michael Müller's *Studies in the History of Moral Theology*[5] confirms the conclusions reached by Janssens. Günthör's very anger makes for poor criticism. Just because we want to discover the core of truth in ecclesiastical traditions, we must trace the influences of each period on these traditions. Without such a laborious effort we shall never escape from the blind alley where we have landed ourselves with our marriage doctrine, according to the words of Patriarch Maximos IV at the Council.

It is definitely not enough to point to the fact that a certain view

---

[4] P. A. Günthör, O.S.B., "Kritische Bemerkungen zu neuen Theorien über die Ehe und eheliche Hingabe," in *Tüb. Theologische Quartalschrift* 144 (1964), pp. 316–50.

[5] Cf. M. Müller, *Die Lehre des hl. Augustinus von der Paradiesesehe und ihre Auswirkung in der Sexualethik des 12. und 13. Jahrhunderts bis Thomas von Aquin*, Studien zur Geschichte der Moraltheologie, Vol. I (Regensburg, 1954); L. Brandl, *Die Sexualethik des hl. Albertus Magnus*, same collection, Vol. II (Regensburg, 1955); J. G. Ziegler, *Die Ehelehre der Pönitentialsummen von 1200–1350*, same collection Vol. IV (Regensburg, 1956).

has prevailed in the Church for several centuries, and particularly not when it is a matter of norms that are not directly given in revelation and on which the Church has made no infallible pronouncement. This is the more relevant when "such traditional and undefined opinions are based on presuppositions that no longer correspond to the increase in our knowledge". [6] In other words, we have no right to impose burdens on people unless "we are absolutely sure that God himself imposes them, and not we or some moral system or some particular document". [7]

3. The invention of, and commercial access to, pills that prevent ovulation have provided present-day discussion with a welcome, concrete point enabling us to deal openly with these theoretical questions. The atmosphere of free discussion in the Council has put aside unnecessary obstacles and made room for the free expression of opinion. This discussion has already shown that much opposition to traditional teaching has sprung from misunderstanding theological terms or from overlooking the factual development of the Church's teaching on particular points. This has led to one-sided and fixed positions that make a businesslike discussion rather difficult. It seems, therefore, important to explain a few presuppositions before we tackle the actual points of the debate.

II

PRELIMINARY POINTS THAT ARE ACCEPTED

1. The right and duty of married couples to exercise their responsibility in limiting births according to number and time have been asserted with increasing clarity in ecclesiastical documents since *Casti Connubii*. The two statements made by Pius XII on October 29 and November 27, 1951 are well known. [8] The Pope

[6] J. M. Reuss, "Eheliche Hingabe und Zeugung," in *Tüb. Theol. Qu.* 143 (1963), p. 455.

[7] H. Küng, "Zusammenfassung eines Referates vor Konzilsvätern," in *Christliche Kultur* 40 (Zurich 28; Nov. 7, 1964).

[8] A.A.S. 43 (1951), pp. 835–54, 855–60; Utz-Groner I, esp. 1073 and 1075.

spoke of the duty of procreation implied in the consummation of marriage (therefore *not* in marriage itself) and said that this duty was not without its limits. Important motives, based in principle on medical, eugenic, economic and social factors, can dispense the partners from this duty in their marital relationship, "also for a long period and even for the duration of the marriage." In the same address he told midwives that there could be circumstances in which it would be "an error and an injustice" to counsel further pregnancy. To the "Fronte della famiglia" he emphasized that the Church shared and understood the real difficulties of married life in contemporary society.

When we glance at the contemporary Catholic literature in German, French and Dutch, we see the clearly accepted Catholic doctrine as expressed by Cardinal Suenens: "The family is the sole judge of the measure in which the creative purpose must be fulfilled".[9] And this decision to be made by each couple on what number of children is "responsible" in their own case, is not a permission, but quite simply a basic duty of married life. That this duty is a matter of principle is not yet sufficiently recognized in practice. From time to time one still meets the opinion that birth control is more or less a concession to those who have proved their goodwill by a certain number of children. This opinion overlooks the completely altered situation in which today's married couples have to consider the matter of procreation.

I do not want to enter into the details of this changed situation. We all know that the sociological revolution which accompanied the industrialization of society led to the disappearance of the large peasant family and to the small family in an urban environment. At the same time, the social structure based on the family

---

[9] Léon-Joseph Cardinal Suenens, *Amour et maîtrise de soi* (Paris, 1960), p. 105. This demand is generally accepted. Cf. L. Salleron, "Le problème de l'optimum familial: Combien faut-il avoir d'enfants?" in *Limitation des naissances et conscience chrétienne* (Ed. Familiales de France, 1950), pp. 81–99. Pastoral letter of the Bishop of Essen: "The Church cannot tell the people how many children they should have. They themselves must ask for light through prayer. They should examine their position before God in order to see this important question in the proper light," in *Kirchliches Amtsblatt für das Bistum Essen* 7 (1964), p. 7. One could refer to many other texts.

(village, relatives, associations) disintegrated and the individual marriage had to stand far more on its own feet. As a result, the partners have to look to each other for security and love far more intensely. Since many work away from home, the partners are no longer united by sharing the same ambition in common labor for their own trade; the stability of their marriage depends therefore only on purely personal values. The facts for all this can be found in a mine of contemporary literature on this subject.[10]

Most important, however, from our point of view is the *progress made in medicine and hygiene.* Here the most striking fact is the sharp decline in infant mortality. This has been reduced to less than 4 percent. This decline in infant mortality has brought with it the fact that natural selection is no longer an operative factor. In the past, constitutionally weak girls often died at an early age; today they practically all reach the childbearing age and early suffer from weariness and other complaints. Older women often unjustly accuse younger women of being oversensitive and rather sorry for themselves; in the old days women had to do with far less prenatal care and did not pay such frequent visits to the doctor.

Such remarks, however, overlook the fact that the situation has changed objectively since little room is left for "natural selection". We should also remember that "natural sterilization" is rare today because of progress in medicine. While formerly a fair number of women became sterile early in life because of puerperal fever, appendicitis or peritonitis, elementary illnesses are so well treated that they rarely cause sterility. This holds even for inflammation of the oviduct, diabetes and other diseases affecting the hormones. In short, modern medicine has succeeded in *ensuring the most favorable conditions for female fertility;* because of this, the decision may often have to be made whether to control this increased capacity for conception by active intervention.

Finally, there is the fact that today women remain fertile for a longer period of years. The latest statistics put the average age for the menopause at $51\frac{1}{2}$, and this means that the problem of

[10] Cf. Leclercq-David, *Die Familie* (Freiburg, 1955), pp. 208–57; B. Häring, *Ehe in dieser Zeit* (Salzburg, 1960), pp. 357–67.

birth control is not limited to young couples but can create serious problems for happily married people in their forties.

All this seems to establish two points.

(a) Thanks to the progress in medicine, a basically healthy marriage must now reckon with a period of twenty-five to thirty years of practically undisturbed fertility. No marriage can cope with this without planning and control. The partners are not justified in shirking their responsibility by leaving it to a wrongly understood divine providence. Our generation, with its experience of war and an uncertain future, certainly needs confidence and trust in God. But this trust in God does not show itself in making divine providence responsible for the number of children, but rather in facing this responsibility which is theirs, consciously and joyfully. (b) The more the developing nations begin to benefit by modern medicine, the more urgent is their need to plan their birth rate.[11]

2. *Marital intercourse should not be considered exclusively as a matter of procreation.* While among the higher animals mating is generally linked with the period of ovulation, the human being is free in the use of intercourse; it is not merely a matter of satisfying a sexual urge but a free expression of love. It is therefore possible that bodily union rarely actually serves the process of procreation in the course of a married life. It must therefore have other values apart from procreation, and this not only in the intention of the partners, but *in itself.* The Church has accepted this by explicitly allowing the intended and planned use of the infertile period (periodic continence). In his address to the Roman Rota (October 3, 1941) Pius XII gave a warning not to view the sex act exclusively as serving procreation but to admit the other values also as true *fines operis* (ends intended by the act). On the other hand, the pope still explicitly maintained that these personal values are subordinated to the end of procreation.

The addresses of October 29, 1951, and May 19, 1956, not only

[11] Cf. J. David, "Soziologische Aspekte zur Frage der Geburtenbeschränkung," in *Orientierung* 27 (Zurich, 1963), VI, p. 65–7; W. Pank, "Ist Geburtenkontrolle ein Gebot der drohenden Ueberbevölkerung?" in *Arzt und Christ* 2 (1963), pp. 89–104.

stress the whole of marriage as a communion of persons, but also the marriage act as the expression of this mutual love and gift of self,[12] yet, once more, not as an end in itself but in relation to marital fertility. It must be admitted that this development under Pius XII has increasingly emphasized the personal values of the marriage act as an objective expression of mutual love, while this particular form of expressing it through the sex act is characterized by the procreative purpose. In this context some speak today of the "creative" rather than of the directly "procreative" meaning of the act.

This development in the official statements of the magisterium seems important. Our understanding of the marriage act provides the norm by which we judge its morality. Nobody will quarrel with this basic principle of Catholic moral theology. Just in those cases where the Bible gives us no factual and individual solutions, the Bible itself points to this basic principle. The faithful obedience that is required of man as redeemed by Christ, must express itself in truth and love. This command of love is not merely addressed to our emotions. It must be worked out in the concrete situation of the human and communal condition. The interpretation of this concrete situation is therefore decisive for any normative statements moral theology cares to make.

Until now, ecclesiastical documents and most moral theology textbooks saw procreation as the only norm of the sex act.[13] Today, even representatives of the Roman school see the norm no longer only in the *actus per se aptus ad generationem et educationem* (the act per se fitted to the procreation and education of children), but also in the *actus per se aptus ad mutuam donationem experimendum* (the act per se fitted to the expression of mutual giving).[14] "The union in the flesh is by its nature ordered toward *both* the

---

[12] "By its nature the marital act is a personal act to be done by both partners in cooperation, and it signifies, because of the nature and specific character of the act, that mutual surrender which makes them one in one flesh, according to Scripture" (Pius XII, Address given on October 29, 1951).

[13] The mutual expression of love has frequently been considered as only a *finis operantis* (the end intended by the one acting). Cf. L. Janssens, *op. cit.*, pp. 807f.

[14] Thus J. Fuchs in his *De Castitate et Ordine sexuali* 3 (Rome, 1963).

expression of marital communion *and*, beyond this, the procreation (and education) of offspring." [15] Few will quarrel with this statement. *The important question is how these two ends of the marriage act are related to each other, and what the nature is of the bond that links them together.* Today this is the question on which the whole discussion turns.

III

VARIOUS INTERPRETATIONS

The key question, then, is: what norms can be derived from the sex act and its purposes, and what are the consequences for the moral assessment of birth control? Some authors base their opinion on fascinating explanations of the essence, meaning and purpose of marriage or on the meaning of sexuality in the Bible. All stress the universal significance of sexuality for mankind. I can only deal indirectly with these questions. I must obviously also be selective. Dozens of French, German and Dutch contributions have reached me, of which many are connected with one another or of which the only differences are a matter of nuances. In spite of justifiable objections to "systematization" of this kind, I am dividing them into three groups because there seem to be three main tendencies.

1. *The Pastoral Tendency*

Those who belong to this group admit willingly that the marriage act in itself includes various purposes, but they maintain that none of these purposes may be effectively excluded whenever the act takes place. They see the act as a metaphysical unity. In the sex act, as in the spoken word, the human person is present and reveals himself, like the spirit in the body. Hence, the biblical description of the marriage act as "knowing" (Gen. 4, 1. 17). This expression shows a profound essential feature of sexual love; in the totality

[15] J. Fuchs, "Moraltheologie und Geburtenregelung," in *Arzt und Christ* 2 (1963), p. 70.

of their sexual union the partners introduce each other into the mystery of their personality in a unique way. "It is an act that experiences the form of the loved one in his bodily being, somewhat similar to the artist's experience, and so enlivens the heart's perception in all man's senses." [16]

In this view the sex act appears also as a symbol of unity. It serves to give shape to the marriage "body", one in the flesh. It realizes what becomes constantly clearer to the two lovers in the measure of their mutual knowledge, namely, their will to become one body. "For this reason a man leaves his father and mother, and clings to his wife, and the two become one flesh" (Gen. 2, 24). It is only possible to leave father and mother and to give up the original shelter within one's family, when one looks for a still deeper union, the "being one flesh", or what Theodor Bovet called the "new marriage person".[17] This ultimate unity must constantly be sought and experienced in the sexual act. As such, the act becomes the objective *expression of mutually giving and receiving love.*

There are many ways of expressing love, like kissing, embracing or holding hands, but the most intense expression is the sexual act. Genuine love, however, does not remain imprisoned within the narrow circle of the loving couple; it transcends the lovers. It is true that it is most directly concerned with the happiness of the beloved; but in realizing this, love becomes fruitful in a way that extends far beyond the loving couple. It is not merely a re-creative element for the spouses, but at the same time a creative element for the family and the world. The biological and physiological act, therefore, which incarnates sexual love, also points to *bodily fertility*. What takes place here is precisely the deed that man will perform when he wishes to procreate in the natural biological way. We may therefore speak of a *primary symbol of procreation*, which by its nature can only be understood in the light of possible fertility. In other words, to unite themselves and to give each other an

---

[16] G. Scherrer, "Die menschliche Geschlechtlichkeit im Lichte der philosophischen Anthropologie," in *Arzt und Christ* 1 (1964), p. 37.
[17] Th. Bovet, *Ehekunde*, I (Tübingen, 1961), pp. 27ff.

intimate token of love would not necessarily require the implanting of the seed. If this is nevertheless intimately connected with the gift of mutual surrender, then it is clear that the act in itself implies more; that it points to possible bodily fertility, even when effective results are only rarely achieved or intended. One should certainly not exclusively concentrate on the bodily and psychological functions, which are presupposed for any sexual encounter, otherwise one would lose sight of the full significance of human sexuality. On the other hand, if sexual love is to be truly realized, this love must be unfolded in the physical and psychological elements of human sexuality.

Now, those that represent the pastoral tendency in this discussion are convinced that the *full beauty and truth* of sexual consummation can only be found when all the levels of meaning are present together in the act. They consider the human act as one, an act where all the meanings converge in one metaphysical whole. They consider it wrong to see in intercourse only the use of a physical organ, now used for this purpose, then for that, as the mouth is used now for speaking, then for eating. The opinion that the sexual organs can be used, now for love and then for procreation, seems in fact unsatisfactory insofar as the whole person is involved in it. The basic law of mutually sharing both spirit and body is important if we wish to understand the specifically human relationship of sex.

These data are presupposed by this group of thinkers when they look for a pastoral solution of the problem: they admit that intercourse must be judged on the basis of all the implied purposes, and stress above all the inner unity of all these values as the dominant "image" in considering marital intercourse. This *dominant image* also implies the *typical character of their "solution"*. This idea of a dominant "image" is somewhat opposed to the idea of "law"—not as if this image did not contain an obligation, but rather in that an "image" does not reduce this obligation to a matter of what is allowed or not allowed, as the law would formulate it. The moral demand to fulfill the values implied in intercourse more and more perfectly does not easily fit into a system of what may I do and what may I not do.

Canon Pierre de Locht has given five radio talks in which he tried to explain this view to his listeners: "From the start I shall try to put the discussion on its true level. It is not a question of what is permitted and what is forbidden, but of positive and negative values (*valeur ou contre-valeur*)".[18] It is a great pity that Catholics and non-Catholics only know our teaching on marriage under the negative aspect of forbidden contraception. Catholic teaching is taken as characterized by what it forbids. For most people Catholic teaching on marriage is distinguished from that of other Christian denominations, such as Anglican or Reformed, by the prohibition of contraceptives. In simple words, it comes to this: others may, we may not. Yet, Catholic teaching is primarily *not at all concerned with a prohibition*. What it is concerned with is the dominant image of true communion in love. This is in general the meaning of Christian ethics that it confronts us with a high ideal in the spirit of the biblical command of love and the Sermon on the Mount.

In this view Catholic teaching sees the dominant image of marital intercourse in the personal act of love, in the fullness of the truth, and including all the levels of meaning harmoniously united in human and personal intercourse. This image implies a vocation for every marriage, but this vocation cannot be simply realized in the way one simply obeys a human law. We are in fact and in all seriousness called to this by God, but there is no simple relationship of justice between the demand and the human ability to cope with it. The human lawgiver has to adjust the law to the citizens' ability to obey it. The possibility to obey the law is one of the basic requirements of a true law. Anyone who tries to compress Christian ethics within the scope of this formula—and unfortunately the attempt is made again and again—suffers from a radical misunderstanding of the position. For Thomas Aquinas all the

[18] Pierre de Locht, *La morale conjugale*, CNPF (Brussels, 1964), 4th talk (pages not numbered).

demands made in the New Testament are nothing but "the letter that kills" if the saving grace of the redemption does not enter into them (*Summa*, Ia IIae, q. 108, a. 2). It is true that God does not ask the impossible, otherwise true guilt would be equally impossible. But for man, so often and in so many ways entangled in the history of the fall while he is in this world, there is nothing left but to do what he can and to pray God to help him with what he cannot yet do. There is a genuine human *non posse* (I am not able) that can only be turned into *posse* (I am able) through long and insistent prayer, and grace.[19]

In this view, Catholic teaching on marriage, based on the kerygma, should be concerned above all with presenting the dominant image of marital love as an illuminating goal. At the same time it must clarify the various failures of the concrete human situation. It could for instance show not merely that divorce is a radical contradict on of the symbol of unity; it can also clearly point out the smaller faults, often hardly noticed. When perhaps a wife prepares herself for her husband by indulging in obscene phantasies, one should not look for the answer in unpersuasive casuistry, laying down what she may and may not do; it would be far more convincing to point to the fullness of the dominant image and so let the weakness explain itself.

The same applies to such lack of mutual consideration or excesses as may be connected with intercourse. All unfulfilled intercourse should clearly tend to the full image. This view would also help to understand why direct contraceptive action is defective where the act of love is concerned. But every marriage begins with being *on the way toward* the goal, and what is decisive is precisely this being on the way: "Whatever difficult situation one may be in, the essential point is *to be on the way*".[20]

The individual couple should always look to the dominant image as if it were a mirror and judge their present condition by what they see there. And it is important to keep an eye on all the values. "It is important, first of all, to go on believing in all those values

[19] Cf. Council of Trent, (Denz. 804).
[20] P. de Locht, *op. cit.*, 5th talk.

proposed by Christian morality, and at the same time to accept that progress is bound to be slow".[21] The spouses are obviously called upon and obliged to leave behind more and more whatever directly contradicts the dominant image; but they are also asked to achieve as many values or aspects of this image as possible at each stage of the way. And this is where the moral decision lies, because in the concrete situation these different values often compete. In this case the moral decision should *not* be based on *whatever may be defective in* the specific shape the act takes here and now, but on the best that can be done in view of the final image. Such a decision must not be considered sinful: in view of the total end aimed at it may be a proof of wisdom. "To know how to accept imperfect behavior as for the moment the least bad approach is to behave wisely and virtuously . . . In this case, to take the line which, with all the necessary generosity, appears to us in conscience the least bad, and therefore the best possible, can be a valid decision, implying no guilt, and even wise".[22]

There is no doubt that Canon de Locht here proposes a "solution" already put into practice for years by kind confessors. Looked at more closely this suggestion provides a new and certainly better way of distinguishing between objective and subjective sin. When, in actual fact, very many Catholics have to make a concrete moral decision about the use of a particular contraceptive method, they are not merely deciding whether to do something that is forbidden, and which is then clouded over by inadequate knowledge or will power. They often have to decide on a difficult choice of what values can be realized or what greater evil can be avoided. This is the way in which our people experience their decision, and insofar as they experience it in this way, one has to agree with Canon de Locht's judgment.

Yet, this pastoral approach by itself is not wholly satisfactory. Josef Fuchs explicitly warns against misunderstanding this so-called "obligation to do what is possible"; it must "not be understood as if, in the meantime, the spouses are not bound to the

[21] *Ibid.*
[22] *Ibid.*

full observance of the order of things. The observance of marital morality belongs to the commands that must be fulfilled and not to those that are aimed at, such as love, which nobody can fulfill in its fullness, and which binds man much more insofar as he is capable of fulfilling it".[23] When there is factual proof that all contraceptive interventions in the act of intercourse are a contradiction of the moral order (which de Locht also apparently presupposes), then the couple is obviously bound to avoid as far as possible whatever contradicts the moral order. But this is not the point here. The partners are, however, equally bound never to do anything that may endanger the body or the life of the other. And when they are at the same time convinced that total abstention will lead to a really serious marital crisis or puts one partner in great moral danger, they have to examine what is the first step to be taken toward implementing the moral order. This is what the supporters of the pastoral solution mean, and nothing else.

As an attitude, chastity is as much an aim as love, and the *ordo caritatis* demands as much respect as the *ordo sexualitatis*. The opposition of love and marital morality is confusing. It leads to the reduction of marital morality to a negative command, and therefore precisely to the error that pastoral-minded theologians seek to avoid. The difficulties of this solution do not lie here. If in fact every contraceptive intervention is wrong, then the pastoral solution is frankly our only chance of putting our morality across in a credible way. The question is much more whether the opposition of married couples to a "merely" pastoral solution does not make it clear that they are not convinced by the reasons given for the objective wrongness of contraception. Most people are willing to accept the basic interpretation of the values of the sex act, but they believe that this interpretation varies according to the purpose. This leads us to another approach with its own supporters.

2. *The Casuistic Approach*

I must make it clear at once that supporters of this approach are not a clearly defined group. Even the word "casuistic" is not

---

[23] J. Fuchs, "Moraltheologie und Geburtenregelung," in *Arzt und Christ* 2 (1963), p. 82.

particularly fortunate as a covering term. I mean to include all attempts at interpreting any *particular* form of contraception as conformable to the Church's teaching with the aid of whatever distinctions are useful. The term covers, therefore, in general all those who ultimately agree that, *apart* from the permitted rhythm method, distinctions must be made between allowable and non-allowable methods of contraception. The third or "radical" group will include those who make no further distinctions about the method. In all this, there is, of course, insofar as the arguments are concerned, room for a certain amount of overlapping.

Among those that follow the casuistic line I mention first those who allow the use of *pills which arrest the ovulation process.* First among these, is Louis Janssens, moral theologian at the University of Louvain.[24] He starts from the fact that the Church today not only admits that parents are responsible for the number of their children, but even demands it in certain circumstances. This makes it necessary to distinguish between what the situation demands of an individual marriage and what of every individual marital act. True responsibility on the part of the couple must exclude all selfish and arbitrary approaches. They should let themselves be guided by factual reasons. Insofar as the individual sex act is concerned, its natural process should be respected (que chaque acte conjugale soit respecté dans sa structure naturelle; p. 816). It is impossible to allow the deliberate perversion of sexual relations (de vicier délibérément les rapports sexuels; p. 816). What does this mean and how can it be substantiated? Does it mean that the sex act may never positively exclude procreation (l'acte conjugale ne peut jamais exclure *positivement* la procréation; p. 817)? Yet, it is positively excluded in the rhythm method. Here it is excluded not only in intention (*finis operantis:* "here and now we do not want procreation") but also in the actual choice of the act. The *choice* here has the *character of a means.*

The inner consent to the completed act necessarily excludes procreation, because the consent is not given to some sexual act in general, but to a precise and deliberate act at a definite moment

[24] L. Janssens, *op. cit.*, pp. 787–826.

while one knows that the act belongs to the infertile period. But the meaning of an act is fully established only when all circumstances are taken into account. In order to assess what is positively wanted or positively not wanted (therefore excluded) in a particular act one has to consider all the concrete conditions that bring it about (il faut examiner le sens de tous les éléments impliqués dans la situation concrète; p. 817). It is precisely the circumstances of time which make the choice of time the means by which procreation is positively excluded.[25] Hence, Janssens concludes that *the decisive reason* for condemning common contraception *cannot lie in the positive and deliberate exclusion of procreation from the marriage act*, because this same exclusion is allowed by the Church in the rhythm method. Janssens maintains, however, that common contraception is not allowed because it perverts (vicier) the sex act. Every marital sex act is by its nature the expression and incarnation of marital love. The structure of this act lies in total mutual surrender. This expression of love is spoiled when a reservation is introduced in the act itself (dans la façon même de le poser; p. 819).

Now, however, supported by the evidence provided by Dr. John Rock[26] and his colleague at Louvain, the gynecologist J. Ferin,[27] Janssens is convinced that the use of anti-ovulation pills does not violate the structure of the act. From this point of view the act is the same whether one uses these pills or the infertile period. The only difference lies in that the rhythm period changes nothing in the cycle (and so there is no question of sterilization), while in the other case ovulation is suppressed. This suppression is seen by many as direct sterilization and therefore disapproved. It depends, according to Janssens, on what is meant by sterilization. If one

---

[25] *Ibid.*, p. 817: "It is precisely this temporal element which turns the use of the safe period into a means for positively excluding reproduction . . . it creates an obstacle of a temporal nature by the exclusive *choice* of intercourse during these periods only, just as contraceptives create an obstacle of spatial nature by putting a material obstruction between the organs of the partners."

[26] Dr. John Rock, *The Time Has Come* (New York: Knopf, 1963).

[27] J. Ferin, "De l'utilisation des médicaments 'inhibiteurs d'ovulation'," in *Eph. Theol. Lov.* 39 (1963), pp. 779–86.

means by this any intervention that sets out deliberately to obstruct the reproductive power,[28] one should be consistent and call the rhythm method also sterilization. But the essence of sterilization is to make any further reproduction impossible by destroying the faculty, though it is in good health.[29] Yet, the occasional suppression of ovulation does not destroy this reproductive power. The swallowing of oral steroids does not cause a disturbance but only a delay in the function, and cannot therefore be identified with sterilization in the true sense.[30] This leads Janssens to the conclusion that birth control through temporary suppression of ovulation is as morally unobjectionable as the use of the rhythm method. To sum up, here once more are his two reasons: the pill *does* exclude conception from the marital act, but this is *not the decisive point*. The suppression of ovulation is not sterilization, because *it does not destroy the capacity to reproduce*.

In a detailed study W. van der Marck, O.P.[31] deals basically with the same question, whether suppression of ovulation by means of progestogene must be considered as sterilization in every case. His answer, however, does not so much rely on scientific presuppositions as on an analysis of the moral act. Illustrating his argument with a reference to the transplantation of an organ he tries to show that an act must always be considered in its totality. That holds also for the use of the pill. The pill and its use are not in themselves bad. The pill can be used for various purposes (sterilization, cure, or birth control). It is simply false to argue that the use of the pill turns sterilization from a means into an end. The use of

---

[28] L. Janssens, *op. cit.*, p. 821: "Any intervention by man, which has as its first aim (*finis operis*) and is meant (*finis operantis*) to injure the reproductive faculty, whether by sterilizing the person or by interfering in the sexual acts."

[29] Note, however, that Pius XII, in his address given at the Congress of hematologists on September 12, 1958 (A.A.S. 50, 1958), called the prevention of ovulation explicitly a temporary sterility, and therefore the not primarily therapeutic action a direct sterilization. One should distinguish the sterilization of the person from the sterilization of the act only. This distinction appears here for the first time in a statement of the magisterium.

[30] Here Janssens keeps close to the arguments of Dr. John Rock.

[31] W. van der Marck, O.P., "Vruchtbaarheidsregeling," in *Tijdschrift voor Theologie* 3 (1963), pp. 378–413.

the pill derives its meaning from its purpose. If the overall purpose of the act is a cure, then the pill is a medicine; when the purpose is to control fertility, then it is a means for birth control; if the intention is to destroy the funct on of reproduction, then it is a means for sterilization. One can only ask whether the use of the pill is good or bad when one has decided what the act, which includes the use of the pill, intends to achieve. Birth control is today not merely allowed by a serious responsibility. If, therefore, the end is good, the use of the pill is also good. According to van der Marck, the rhythm method is equally concerned with a positive regulation of fertility. This does not prevent it from being allowed, since it does not affect *sexual union*.

The same conclusion is reached by Th. C. J. Beemer.[32] This author is of the opinion that the Church's teaching has a too narrow and biological idea of fertility. One ought to distinguish between *actual* and *integral fertility;* the idea of sterilization would then be understood as applying only to the destruction of integral fertility.

The previously mentioned three theologians were mainly concerned with whether the use of anti-ovulation pills is allowed or not. J. M. Reuss, suffragan bishop and director of the seminary of Mainz, tackles the problem in a broader fashion.[33] Reuss, too, begins by stressing that the specifically human sexuality and marriage must be seen as a whole. Copulation must not be treated as an isolated action but must be seen in conjunction with the marriage that encompasses it. Most married people today cannot think of a harmonious relationship without the joy of full intercourse. When, therefore, the bodily and personal union of man and wife is in fact so indispensable to a harmonious relationship that to renounce it would seriously affect this necessary relationship, it would be wrong to give up intercourse. When, at the same time, it would be imperative in certain circumstances not to have

[32] Th. C. J. Beemer, "Beinvloeding van de vruchtbaarheid door de progestatieve hormon-preparaten," in *Katholiek artsenblad* 42 (1963), pp. 7–12.

[33] J. M. Reuss, "Eheliche Hingabe und Zeugung," in *Tüb. Theologische Quartalsschrift* 143 (1963), IV, pp. 454–76.

any more children, then the only solution would be to "maintain intercourse in a way that cannot lead to procreation" (p. 469).

This is basically what the rhythm method tries to achieve. But what happens when the partners cannot dispose of enough "safe" days? Should then the possibility be created for unproductive intercourse? Reuss admits that "to use safe days is not the same as to introduce infertility" (p. 471). But he also sees the close connection between the safe period and other methods insofar as man's inner activity is concerned. The safe period covers a series of human actions, outward deeds and inner decision. Intercourse as such is not rendered incapable of reproduction, but through his intervention, man deprives intercourse of the necessary conditions for reproduction (the exact connection of intercourse with its biological concomitants). "Thus, by using the safe period, man prevents intercourse from reaching procreation" (p. 471).

Insofar as the intention is concerned, there is no relevant difference between the two types of activity. Is it possible to discover a more significant moral difference under some other angle? Hardly from the point of view of bodily integrity: there is no biological and physiological factor that can never be interfered with under any circumstances. Could it be found in the close connection with the act of intercourse? Reuss distinguishes here between interventions in biological and physiological factors *connected with* intercourse and interventions in the *fulfillment* of intercourse (p. 473).

The first kind (interventions in the sex act as such) he rejects emphatically. So the question only concerns interventions in the fulfillment of intercourse, which, like the safe period, do not affect the act itself, but, again like the safe period, make it possible to let intercourse run its course without the possibility of procreation. Such an intervention "is not forbidden under all circumstances unless one maintains that it is so different from other biological and physiological factors in its relation to the *copula* (intercourse) that it can never be allowed. But this would imply the definite certainty that procreation is so essential to every act of intercourse that man could under no circumstances do anything to prevent it"

(p. 473). But since man is, in fact, allowed to do so by freely using the safe period, it is obvious that intercourse is not essentially linked to procreation.

Reuss does not mention any concrete methods he considers acceptable. This is not a matter for theologians: their function is to develop the basic principle in a critical manner. According to Reuss' distinction in principle between interventions in the act of intercourse and interventions in the purpose of intercourse the suspension of ovulation must be considered as allowable, at least when the safe period fails. If for one reason or another there were an objection to the use of hormonal means, one might wonder whether it would not logically follow from Reuss' distinction to allow the artificial closure of the mouth of the uterus in the woman. This, too, would be a means that would not directly affect the mutual surrender of the act but would simply be applied in view of the act as a whole. I must make it clear, however, that Reuss himself does not draw this conclusion.

The positions so far dealt with in this second group all have this in common that any direct intervention in the act of intercourse is rejected, but not a temporary sterilization in view of voluntary intercourse.[34] These theologians do not deny that the procreative purpose is part of the inner meaning of sexual intercourse; they doubt, however, whether the suspension of certain biological and physiological conditions in view of the act as a whole prevents the genuine expression of mutual surrender more than the deliberate choice of safe days for intercourse. In spite of some differences in the argument,[35] all appeal to the moral recognition of the safe period.

This forces us to examine the question whether this comparison with the safe period is justified. If we consider the naked fact of an infertility brought about by a time factor, the comparison does not

[34] Interventions in connection with rape are not taken into consideration here.

[35] While Janssens holds that the effective prevention of reproduction in an isolated act, as here indicated, does not by itself decide the morality of the act, Reuss tries to justify this prevention in the process of the physical act (*opus naturae*) as opposed to the human act (*actus humanus*) by appealing to the principle of marriage as a whole.

hold. In spite of the most specious diagnosis of ovulation, the infertility of the safe period is an *object* (*volitum*) but not an *effect* (*voluntarium*) of the human will.[36] But the suspension of ovulation produces an infertility which is undoubtedly the result of human intervention.[37] According to the recognized principles of morality man is only and always responsible for the effect (*voluntarium*). In fact, this was the reason why the safe period was freely allowed.

It was always maintained that man may (perhaps must) refuse to have a child; he may (and even must) freely choose his time for intercourse; but he may not effectively frustrate procreation. Reuss and Janssens are well aware of this; yet, they persist in comparing the methods on the basis of responsibility. This responsibility lies in fact in the deliberate choice. Systematic use of the safe period does not merely imply the free calculation of the time when intercourse shall take place: this time is carefully *chosen*. There is a difference between a simple choice and a careful selection. The *deliberate care* with which ovulation is avoided corresponds to the activity through which it is suspended. And I must admit that, presuming we take things seriously, there seems to be no serious ground for a significant moral difference between the two methods; it is certainly not such that a thinking man would have to choose between them as between a grave moral fault and a morally good action.[38] In any case, the discussion between professors of moral theology shows that here the intellectual ability of those who have to live this moral teaching wears rather thin. The ethical significance, at least, of the various elements and moments that make up the process of intercourse urgently need definite clarification.

According to B. Häring[39] it appears that in Rome the question

[36] So far Günthör's criticism is quite correct. Cf. *op. cit.*, *Tüb. Theologische Quartalsschrift* 144 (1964), III, p. 337.

[37] At all events, this is still always considered the main effect of the prevention of ovulation. Moreover, there is still the opinion which holds that the pill can also prevent the implantation of a fertilized ovulum in the endometrium. Cf. G. A. Hauser, "Erfahrungen mit Ovulationshemmern," in *Médecine et Hygiène* 22 (May 27, 1964), pp. 479–81.

[38] Cf. F. Böckle, "Verantwortete Elternschaft," in *Wort und Wahrheit* 19 (Oct. 1964), p. 584.

[39] B. Häring, "La théologie et la pilule contraceptive," in *La Documentation Catholique* 46 (July 19, 1964), pp. 891ff.

is seriously examined whether suspension of ovulation must always be regarded as direct sterilization, even when it leads to birth control. The thought that every woman goes through an infertile period with cyclic regularity is not wholly foreign even to Roman theologians. And they wonder whether at least in all cases where the infertile period cannot be diagnosed or applied, suspension of ovulation is not a matter of producing some kind of infertile period instead of leading to sterilization. This much can be considered even on the basis of the traditional moral teaching that concentrates on individual actions.[40] To many it appears the only solution possible today. To us these last considerations seem to take on the aspect of quibbling and I am afraid that in this way we present a still less credible picture to the world. The efforts made by Reuss and Janssens seem far more positive, but they have to be thought through to the end and they should complement each other. This is what the third group of theologians is trying to do.

[40] Cf. G. Ermecke, in KNA-Dokumentation, n. 33 (August 12, 1964). He tries to solve the problem by appealing only to the principle of the indirect effect. Ermecke aims at an extension of the principle of totality. Up till now this principle was only applied when an intervention was absolutely necessary in order to preserve the individual's life or to protect from heavy and lasting injury. Ermecke wonders whether this principle should not apply also to the relation between the individual and the community, for instance in the case "when members should adjust themselves to the needs of the whole community". On the basis of the principle of "double effect" these interventions should not only eliminate danger from individual intercourse but should always foster the common good as in the case of uncontrollable overpopulation or the prevention of hereditary diseases. In a recent article, "Eheliche Hingabe und Zeugung" in *Scholastik* XXXIX (1964), pp. 528–57, Klaus Demmer, MSC., developed similar thoughts. Demmer considers the use of the pill debatable if this pill does not suppress ovulation but only checks it. He would agree with an extension of the cycle. For the rest, he starts with an excellent explanation of the right approach to sexual morality, but then commits a disastrous *petitio principii* when he summarily interprets human sexuality as love (*genericum*) tending to procreation (*specificum*). Love as a personal relationship cannot be subordinated to another end: the person is an end in itself. The child is at most an accessory end of personal human love. The specific difference (a constitutive ontological element) of sexual love is only the "becoming one flesh" (Gen. 2, 24). This means that love may never be excluded from the sex act, but that on the other hand the *generatio prolis* may be excluded from the individual act of intercourse for moral reasons, although love as a whole is intimately connected with the function of procreation.

3. *The Radical Approach*

I am not speaking here of a kind of radical theology; I use the term "radical" with reference to the root (*radix*) of our problem, and I count as belonging to this group all those who are convinced that sexual morality must be understood afresh from the very roots, *i.e.*, from our concept of nature. It is not lack of respect for what has been taught and written for centuries on the purpose of marriage, which inspires these thinkers. It is rather the understanding of the real historicity of both man and his knowledge, which has driven many theologians to the conviction that a concept of nature based on what men and animals have in common (*id quod natura omnia animalia docet*) cannot serve as a basis for a morality of *human* sexuality.

No one quarrels with the twofold traditional principle of Catholic moral theology of *secundum caritatem et secundum rationem* (to judge according to love and according to reason). On the contrary, the theologians struggle to understand the inner bond of these two factors and they see this union in the relation between love and truth. "Love rejoices with the truth" (1 Cor. 13, 6) and therefore we must "practice the truth in love" (Eph. 4, 15). The Christian's obedience in faith finds its fulfillment in love. The command of love radically affects the whole of the law. Christ has fulfilled the law in the love of his self-surrender, and in his love we are called to share in this fulfillment. He has empowered us to bear witness to his love by realizing it in the concrete situation that presents itself to us. This is what decides Christian morality: to give shape to love in the reality of our fully human, creaturely, bodily and social existence. Since we ourselves are subject to the process of history and our knowledge of ourselves as well as of the world is historically conditioned, we must constantly reexamine the meaning of our existence if we want our love to be realistic. The obligatory elements in our relationships are determined by this interpretation of our existence in the world. This does not mean that these elements are simply "invented" or "made up" by man. They are attempts to explain a reality that contains in its own existence a transcendental obligation. Catholic theology knows that it is obliged before God, from whom man receives all knowledge of the truth, to look for God's continuous creative act in the created reality and to understand in what direction his creative will is leading us.

These basic thoughts form the matter of a study in depth by E. Schillebeeckx.[41] In the first part he deals with the principles underlying the question of whether the norms of morality can change. One should start from the fact that all human knowledge is a matter of perspective, *i.e.*, it is a view of the truth from a particular point so that every insight can grow and become more complete (p. 7). One and the same significant factor can be illuminated from various directions so that there are different ways of understanding it and these different views can complement each other. We must, therefore, draw a clear distinction between the truth in itself and the truth insofar as man possesses it. Truth in itself (ultimately God) does not change; even our affirmation of the truth does not really change. What does change is the perspective along which we approach the truth. The more we are conscious of this perspective character of our knowledge, the less danger there is of falling into relativism because the more perspectives we have the closer we come to absolute truth. The author then proceeds to give an historical survey of the changes in perspective that have affected the teaching about marriage.

Chrysostom, Augustine, the theologians of the school of St. Victor, the Scholastics, Pius XI (*Casti Connubii*) and H. Doms have all spoken of "the same material subject, marriage, but from formally different aspects". The question about the primary and secondary ends of marriage is typically dualistic, whether the primary end is seen in the child or in living together (p. 11); this corresponds to an *analytical approach to marriage*. But *in the concrete* marriage is about a human *whole*. In this human wholeness the spiritual element is no doubt primary, but it is embodied in

[41] E. Schillebeeckx, O.P., "De Natuurwet in verband met de katholieke huwelijksopvatting," in *Jaarboek der katholieke Theologen 1961* (Hilversum, 1963), pp. 5–51.

the bodily element. The question, therefore, whether the child or the living together of two persons is the first aim of marriage loses its meaning in this perspective.

The solution can only be expressed in terms of "incarnation". In this view there is only *one aim in marriage*, which is *complex* because human reality itself is complex. This aim is the fullness of two persons sharing one life, with its two dimensions, namely, mutual responsibility for each other's personal existence *and* shared responsibility for the personal existence of the children. In this way Schillebeeckx shows that conceptualism (the attempt to limit oneself to the analysis of an idea without constant reference to the growing understanding of concrete reality) leads to the crudest kind of relativism, because it absolutizes one given perspective. This is the more dangerous when it claims to represent the absolute truth.[42]

In the second part of his study Schillebeeckx deals with what is called "physicism", that is, the traditional opinion that the biological elements of an act have a normative value for moral behavior. If one wishes to follow the opinion of Ulpian, who sees the norm for sexual relationships in what man and animal have in common, one might as well prove with our present knowledge that masturbation and homosexuality are also features that man and animal have in common (p. 14). *The biological aspect of nature cannot be erected as such into a norm of morality. Only an overall anthropological view of nature can provide the grounds for ethical investigations.*

The exact sciences can only show us the various biological possibilities contained in sexuality (its polyvalent meaning). The anthropological view is only concerned with those possibilities in which the human spirit can embody itself; "in which, however, it must embody itself after a human and therefore moral fashion" (p. 24). How this should be brought about (*e.g.*, as expression of love, with personal happiness and the unfolding of human values as

[42] Schillebeeckx makes it very clear that, obviously, the data of revelation must not be understood "in perspective" in the same way.

the necessary consequences) is beyond the scope of science and belongs to theology. Here lies the relevance for morality; only the *humanization* of bioligical possibilities in the light of a whole way of life is morally significant. The integration, therefore, of biological and sexual possibilities in a way of life is therefore subject to what the Church and moral theology decide. It is in this light that the Church's rejection of contraception must be seen and interpreted.

Although there is here no question of a pronouncement *ex cathedra*, Schillebeeckx is of the opinion that "we are in fact faced with the universal teaching of the bishops of the world, so that we cannot go back on it. Moreover, it is unthinkable that in such a vitally important question the Church would in fact err in teaching something that has not been declared infallibly" (p. 25). The decisive point, therefore, is what constitutes the *real core of the Church's position*. And here Schillebeeckx comes to the conclusion that what is absolutely irrevocable in the Church's teaching is *the impossibility of combining the essence of marriage and the basic decision to lead a married life with the positive exclusion of the child*, in whatever way this exclusion is brought about (safe period or contraception). The basic decision to accept the married state with the exclusion of the child is radically opposed to the specific nature of marital union. However, the question remains open whether the Church wants to state in this way that all the values of married life must be fully expressed in every single act.

The theology of the last twenty years has made the real, though not adequate, distinction between the moral norms for married life as a whole and the individual act of consummation. The real *actus humanus* of marriage is expressed in the basic decision to enter the married state, so that the individual act of intercourse is but an *actus humanus* insofar as it shares in this overall decision. "The isolated act cannot always realize to the full all that belongs to a person's basic conviction through an *actus humanus* that lies on a deeper level than the isolated act" (p. 29). These distinctions have not yet been embodied in ecclesiastical documents. The author also thinks that the Church can obviously extend her condemnation of contraception in a superficial way to the *actus humanus* in face of these distinctions. "I only mean that one cannot attribute to the Church an assertion that she has not made and cannot make while she has not yet accepted this distinction between the state of married life and the isolated act. Theologians who maintain that the Church's teaching applies to both these factors, may be right, but in doing so they extend the bearing of the Church's position" (p. 29). Such an extension must be put to the account of the theologians and is as valid as its proof.

The Church as such has made no such pronouncement. This much is certain: one cannot bluntly say that "intercourse must not be frustrated". As such, this assertion is incorrect and "physicist". According to the anthropological principle one should say: Not intercourse as such, but intercourse as an *actus humanus* must not be frustrated. And then one has to remember that the *actus humanus* is not a specific moment that can be detached from the human person as a whole, but one element within the fullness of the person in the wholeness of his life and basic intentions (pp. 30–31).

Au fond Schillebeeckx brings together two points of view that complement each other: first the distinction between a physicist and an anthropological approach to the act, and then, within this anthropological approach, the distinction between the overall intention and the individual action. The physicist approach prevails among theologians; this is obvious from the recent controversy about the pill. When, for instance, they argue that direct sterilization is *secundum naturam* insofar as nature itself provides this infertile period, they show a typically physicist approach. The anthropological approach shows more in the discussion about sterilization in a case of rape. Insofar as the ecclesiastical magisterium is concerned one can in no case conclude that there is a general prohibition of every intervention in the act of intercourse on the biological and physiological level. When such an intervention is in harmony with the overall intention of the married state and no definite harm is done to any personal value, it should not be considered immoral.

J. David, S.J., comes to much the same conclusions.[43] He is particularly opposed to isolating the act of intercourse from marriage as a whole. This act must always be seen in the light of marriage as whole and its fulfillment in the light of the child. As an institution, marriage is responsible for procreation. This command of the creator is fulfilled when the marriage bond includes fertility and fulfills it as far as possible. The isolated act then serves the procreation and education of children directly or indirectly (through the deepening of marital love) within marriage as a whole.[44]

To the objection that the intention to procreate must *per se* be present in every individual act, David and others reply that nature itself separates fertility from the act and in no way demands that every act should lead to reproduction. Here David opposes a metaphysical view of the act in itself (as symbol of procreation) which

---

[43] J. David, "Zur Frage der Geburtenregelung," in *Theologie der Gegenwart* 7 (1964), II, pp. 71–9. See also the reactions to this article *ibid.* 7 (1964), IV, pp. 211–31.

[44] This reasoning was given more weight by the intervention of Cardinal Léger in the Council on October 28, 1964 when he supported it in the following terms: "The schema treats well of procreation as an aim of marriage where it emphasizes that this must be dealt with intelligently and boldly. It should be added, however, that this duty concerns less the individual act than marriage as a whole. . . . married love which is human, *i.e.*, embraces both body and soul, must particularly be put forward as a true aim of marriage, as something that is good in itself and has its own laws and demands. On this point the schema looks timid. There is little advantage in avoiding the idea of *finis secundarius* if love is after all still understood as only tending to procreation. This important matter demands that we lay down clear principles . . . If this love is not clearly recognized as an aim of marriage, the relations between the partners will remain obscure. The partners do not look on each other merely as procreators, but also as persons who love each other for each other's sake." It is not enough to lay down the teaching about the aims of the married state in order to solve the practical and theological problems; one should go to the heart of the matter and explain the aim of the individual act with the help of general principles. One must maintain that marital union also aims at fostering the mutual love of the partners, and this aim must be seen as a *finis operis* (the aim of the actual action) "which is legitimate in itself, even if it does not tend to procreation". The Council should therefore frankly recognize both ends of marriage as good and holy.

rejects the purely biological approach, but he does so with definitely biological and physicist arguments.[45]

It is better to point, with Schillebeeckx, to the inconsistency of the so-called metaphysical approach which constantly tries to defend its anthopological position with biological and physiological arguments (*e.g.*, by referring to the ejaculation that accompanies every act). It is right to point, as David does, to the wide differences between man and animal in this context. For man, intercourse is not linked with an ovulation period; this is a peculiarly anthropological factor. In this human perspective the objective values of intercourse do not run parallel. This act is in a very different way the expression of love and symbol of reproduction. The act can always express love, but is frequently but an ineffective symbol of reproduction.

That is why it is worth observing that, in the case of *man*, the *aspect* of reproduction can be lacking; it is not merely a matter of the *life force* missing an *opportunity* for reproduction. I mean that the fact of unreproductive intercourse under certain biological conditions does not prove that we may bring about this unreproductiveness. We can only make progress in this argument when we can show that a married *human person* can lose the right to further reproduction, in other words, that he is not allowed to reproduce in certain circumstances. The question then arises whether in these circumstances he may intervene in the biological and physiological process of the act. This is, in my opinion, the real core of the problem: should a person yield to the biological aspect of an act, or should *this* biological aspect of the act be subordinated to the moral purposes of a human person? When the human being must not wish for another child, should he act "as if" in the factual process of the act (*id quod fit*), or should he change the biological process, or should he renounce the act altogether? The answer to

---

[45] Perhaps David's reference here should be looked at as an *argumentum ad hominem:* according to present knowledge the act never is a one-sided performance aimed at procreation, at least not in the case of human beings. In the great majority of cases intercourse has also other functions, even biologically speaking, which give meaning to the act, and this not accidentally but essentially.

these questions will vary according to whether one subscribes to an ontology dominated by things, or to an ontology dominated by the person, the only ontology that fully accepts the analogy of being.[46]

The philosopher, Walter Brugger, argues consistently from the point of view of a personalist ontology.[47] According to him, one can no longer speak of an arbitrary division of the ends of marriage when one end (reproduction) is excluded for objective reasons. The question then becomes with what means the other ends can still be saved. Traditional teaching allows then only the safe period and excludes any sterilization as contrary to nature. Whether this position can be maintained depends, according to Brugger, on one's concept of "nature". Does one mean by "nature" the physiological processes of the body with their own built-in purpose, or does one mean the way in which man as a whole is related to his final and constitutive end? The latter meaning is the only one relevant to morality. A disturbance of nature in the physical and physiological sense is not simply identical with a disturbance of nature in the metaphysical sense. It is true that contraception goes against the physiological nature of the act, but "this does not necessarily mean that the will to use contraception also goes against human nature in the metaphysical sense, because here one can no longer ignore the morality or immorality of the action." This means that the morality of the method used when birth control is morally required does not depend on whether one "merely" uses temporary infertility or whether one creates such a temporary or actual infertility. (This distinction is in itself typically physicist!)

The only morally relevant decision here lies in the relation to personal love, of which the sex act must always be the symbolic expression. And here we meet again the supporters of the second approach, Janssens and Reuss, although on a wholly different level. For, basically, Janssens and Reuss start with the traditional moral evaluation of the act, and then doubt whether this evaluation can be based on the consummation of the act. But the supporters

---

[46] Cf. J. B. Lotz, *Scholastik* 38 (1963), p. 336.
[47] W. Brugger, S.J., in a stenciled manuscript.

of the third group base this evaluation in principle on the person and his original decision. Something like this can be discerned in Reuss' treatment of the right to intervene, and it certainly hovers in the background of Janssens' argument when he evaluates the act by its symbolic value for the total mutual surrender. But I have a certain hesitation when this evaluation is again one-sidedly linked with the process of intercourse. In any case, the danger of physicism is getting closer.

Is closure of the uterine orifice against the expression of love? Such questions cannot be decided merely by the act of intercourse. We would be driving out the devil with the help of Beelzebub. The third group of theologians seem more consistent here. They demand of the partners that they have the serious intention to have children in the overall plan for their married life; they demand a serious and morally acceptable motive for excluding fertility from a specific individual act, and insofar as the method is concerned, they require in a general way that it should be compatible with considerate behavior and love because intercourse should be the expression of this love. Here these theologians refer to the supporters of the pastoral approach. The constant realization of love shows man his basic weakness and his dependence on God's grace. He knows that the road is long, but, if honestly pursued, not easier than obediently following a precisely indicated method as has been done so far. There is no need to fear a decline in sexual morality when the faithful begin to take this road of the considerate and noble art of loving. For the moment we must patiently and confidently await the Church's judgment. The Pope has made this problem a matter of his own conscience. This, however, does not dispense theologians from pursuing their labor nor the laity from enlightening their consciences and taking their decisions accordingly.

Enda McDonagh / *Maynooth, Ireland*

not for the Refectory

Recent English Literature on the Moral Theology of Marriage

Much of the abundant literature in English on this subject is irrelevant to this survey, as it is either popularization or translation. There remains an increasing volume of useful theological material, some of which in recent years has moved out of the conventional manual framework to adopt the more perilous but ultimately more rewarding biblical, theological and existential approach. And one of the remarkable features of marriage theology in the latest developments has been the contributions of articulate lay people.

The survey takes as its starting point the year 1958. In that year Pius XII died, and with his death and the election of John XXIII it could be said that one ecclesiastical and theological era ended and another began. As far as the theology of marriage is concerned, in that year Pius XII's Address to the Hematologists condemning the new oral contraceptive and the Anglican Lambeth Conference's acceptance of family-planning "in such ways as are mutually acceptable to husband and wife in Christian conscience", provide in the English-speaking world obvious points of climax to a period of hectic writing and thinking. This period began in 1930 with Lambeth's first real concession to contraception, followed by Pius XI's authoritative condemnation of it in *Casti Connubii*—all in the very year of the Ogino-Knaus discoveries of the fertile-infertile periods in the female cycle.

BIBLICAL AND SACRAMENTAL BASIS

For a long time the theology of marriage ignored to a large extent the primary source of theological reflection—Scripture. This has been remedied somewhat in recent years. A useful survey in English of the scriptural teaching on marriage is provided by Wilfrid Harrington, O.P.[1] Father Harrington moves from the prototype of marriage as outlined in Genesis 1 and 2, containing the "essential doctrine of marriage", to the prophetic image of marriage for the covenant between God and his People with its personal commitment in love. He regards "The Canticle of Canticles" as a poetic celebration of human love, which, consecrated in New Testament marriage, expresses "the union of Christ and his Church".

The transforming effect on marriage resulting from its association with the sanctifying union of Christ and the Church, making it both a (partial) realization and sign of this union, finds theological expression in the Church's doctrine on the sacrament of marriage. Despite the obvious impossibility of having an effective Christian theology of marriage living (a moral theology of marriage) without close consideration of its sacramental as well as its biblical dimension, very little attention has been given to marriage as a sacrament. The dogmatic manuals refer to the moral manuals that are dominated by contractual and legal elements. Donal Flanagan provides a welcome introduction to such a study in "The Sacrament of Marriage."[2]

The relevance of the sacrament for Christian living is tackled by Fr. Flanagan in his discussion of sacramental grace,[3] which, on the basis of *Casti Connubii*, must include something more than the usually mentioned sanctifying grace plus title to actual grace, in

[1] "Marriage in Scripture," in *The Meaning of Christian Marriage*, Enda McDonagh (ed.), papers of the Maynooth Union Summer School (Dublin, 1963), pp. 14–35. Cf. J. McKenzie, *The Two-Edged Sword* (Milwaukee, 1956), pp. 90ff.

[2] "The Sacrament of Marriage," in *The Meaning of Christian Marriage*, Enda McDonagh (ed.). Cf. J. Keens, S.J., *The Theology of Marriage* (New York, 1964), pp. 197f.

[3] *Op. cit.*, pp. 46–53.

fact, "something in the nature of infused habits—supernaturally conferred capacities to think, will and act as married and as married in Christian marriage". These operate in a restorative way, renewing the harmony upset by original sin, as St. Thomas and many Scholastics would have thought, and effecting in a truly profound way a *remedium concupiscentiae*.

THE INSTITUTION OF MARRIAGE

Although the biblical and sacramental undertaking of marriage as well as human experience would suggest a greater reality, the moral theologians have tended to concentrate on the contractual aspect of marriage. In this century, some voices have been raised in criticism of this. One of the few among the English-speaking Catholics has been that of Archbishop Beck of Liverpool.[4] He feels that the emphasis on contract has weakened people's grasp of marriage as "a permanent and indissoluble union", and expresses great sympathy with Professor Georges Renard and his views on marriage as an institution that is more than a contract. Here he is reechoing the puzzlement that many married people feel about the canonical description of marriage, which has become for so many moral theologians the only, or at least, the prevailing description.

Efforts are being made to develop a theology of marriage that has the biblical, sacramental and existential qualities necessary and at the same time preserves the essential obligations of the law. On the other hand, some of the exponents of the conventional framework are trying to fill out the bare bones of the law and to treat the fuller human and Christian aspects as well. These two approaches find expression in the current literature in English and their difference emerges both in the initial approach to the nature of marriage and in their consequent treatment of the ends of marriage. Since both the nature and purposes of marriage are intimately related, it will be convenient to treat them together, discussing first the more legal and then the more personal, theological approach.

[4] "The Contemporary Crisis," in *The Meaning of Christian Marriage*, pp. 6, 10.

THE NATURE AND PURPOSES OF MARRIAGE

1. The Legal Approach

The most comprehensive, fair-minded and best work of this kind is undoubtedly *Contemporary Moral Theology, Vol. II, Marriage Questions*[5] by John Ford and Gerald Kelly. It might seem unfair to describe it as a legal work but the discussion on this topic dominated by the legal realities of contract, bond and rights and the use of biblical and sacramental data is minimal. The terminology and scale of values is much closer to the code of canon law and the canonists than to the Bible and the theologians. Yet there is a wealth of clear and rewarding thought, once the limits of the approach are recognized and accepted.[6]

For them "the essence of marriage is a bond of the juridical order"[7] and "the ends of marriage are its essential meaning". In elaborating on the essence of marriage as "the essential marriage right and the essential marriage relation",[8] they distinguish between the fundamental right and proximate right. This distinction is developed very effectively in explaining how the radical relationship of marriage remains, for instance, even though one partner, for example, may have lost the proximate right to the act of intercourse. For "the marriage bond consists in a right to the acts by which the ends are achieved".[9] The distinction between fundamental and proximate right shown to be necessary in this way, has hitherto been implicit in theological writing and judicial decisions.

With the code, they distinguish the essential ends of marriage into primary (procreation and rearing of children) and secondary (mutual help and remedy for concupiscence).[10] To the secondary ends of the canon they add with *Casti Connubii* the fostering of conjugal love as not identical with either of these and they devote

---

[5] John C. Ford and Gerald Kelly, *Contemporary Moral Theology, Vol. II, Marriage Questions* (Newman Press, 1963).

[6] For a sound but hard criticism of their approach, cf. D. Callahan, "Authority and the Theologian," in *Commonweal* (New York, June 5, 1964), pp. 319ff.

[7] Ford and Kelly, *op. cit.*, p. 53; cf. also pp. 42–7.

[8] *Ibid.*, pp. 57ff.

[9] *Ibid.*, p. 57.

[10] *Ibid.*, p. 47.

one whole chapter to discussing it.[11] For them, primary means "more important", but they do insist that both primary and secondary are essential to marriage,[12] so that the exclusion of the (fundamental) right to any of the secondary ends, *e.g.*, conjugal love would invalidate the marriage. It is not the absence of love, but the absence of the fundamental right and corresponding obligation that would invalidate.

Their explicit inclusion of conjugal love as an essential purpose of marriage and not reducible to mutual help and *remedium concupiscentiae* (remedy for concupiscence) is obviously important. Love they define as "the virtue by which man and wife wish to communicate to each other the benefits proper to marriage",[13] which are "the acts of the conjugal life, all acts by which the essential ends of marriage are realized".[14] Foremost among these is intercourse, and then come all the other acts of mutual help. In an age in which "instinctive impulses and unconscious attraction" have been confused with love, their desire to emphasize the rational character of love is understandable but gives an impression of abstract rationality rather than personal commitment.

On the relations between the ends or purposes of marriage, they are clear and unambiguous. The secondary ends including conjugal love are essentially subordinated to the primary and objectively less important.[15] And so "the procreative finality of sterile marriages as of fertile marriages is more fundamental to them than their other purposes".[16]

2. *The Personal, Theological Approach*

Despite their clarity and humanity, Frs. Ford and Kelly (and dozens of lesser theologians) are operating within such narrow confines in concepts, terminology and sources that their most persuasive writing shows signs of strain. Other thinkers have tried

[11] *Ibid.*, pp. 103–26.
[12] *Ibid.*, pp. 49ff. Cf. chapter 5: "The Essential Character of the Secondary Ends," pp. 75–102.
[13] *Ibid.*, p. 110.
[14] *Ibid.*, p. 114.
[15] *Ibid.*, p. 127ff.
[16] *Ibid.*, p. 136.

to get behind the canons, the moral manuals and even the encyclicals to the primary realities in Scripture and in man's sexuality as created by God.

An interesting example of a very personalist essay on marriage is that of Dietrich von Hildebrand.[17] For him, marriage has a meaning and value in itself and not only as an end.[18] This meaning derives from its character as "the closest loving union between man and woman,[19] now elevated by Christ to a sacrament, so that "only in Christ and through Christ can the spouse live up to the full glory and depth at which this love by its very nature aspires".[20] And to this love union "God has confided the coming to being of a new man, a cooperation with his divine creativity".[21] But the link is not that of simple instrumental causality—as a knife is designed for cutting and derives all its meaning from it. Marriage has its own value antecedently and is linked to procreation by the "Principle of Superabundance", somewhat as knowledge is linked to action.[22]

The sensitive understanding of sexual and married love that von Hildebrand displays cannot be captured in a summary. However, his introduction of the "Principle of Superabundance" to link marriage as a union of love with procreation seems artificial and unnecessary.

Bernard Häring's description of marriage in his paper "Community of Love"[23] (and touched on elsewhere)[24] reveals some of the divine reflection in marriage that might have been expected

[17] Dietrich von Hildebrand, "Marriage and Overpopulation," in *Thought* 36 (1961), pp. 81–100.

[18] *Ibid.*, p. 82.

[19] *Ibid.*, p. 90.

[20] *Ibid.*, p. 91.

[21] *Ibid.*, p. 92.

[22] *Ibid.*, pp. 93f.

[23] Bernard Häring, "Community of Love," in *The Meaning of Christian Marriage* (see footnote 1), pp. 62–79.

[24] Cf. "Christian Marriage and Family Planning," (Fr. John A. O'Brien interviews Fr. Bernard Häring) in *The Problem of Population* (Notre Dame, 1964); B. Häring, "Responsible Parenthood," in *Commonweal* (New York, June 5, 1964), pp. 323ff.; "Fr. Häring's Views": Extracts from *The Guardian* and *Catholic Herald* (May, 1964) in *The Pill*, Leo Pyle (ed.), pp. 150–64 (London, 1964).

from its biblical and sacramental basis. As God is love, so married love (which is in germ, parental love) manifests God and God's love. From this standpoint, he makes a valuable contribution to the perennial controversy about the relation between the ends of marriage. The code mentions as secondary ends only *mutuum adjutorium* (mutual help) and *remedium concupiscentiae* (remedy for concupiscence). But neither of these is love (a point also made by Frs. Ford and Kelly) [25] and married love itself is not primarily an end or *finis* or *causa finalis* but source of marriage, a *causa formalis*.[26] It is the mutual love, their choice of and commitment to each other that brings the couple together and forms the marriage. Insofar as the marriage will of its nature tend to develop this love, it may be spoken of in this sense as an end of marriage. And the proper description of procreation and education that he calls "the service of new life" would be the *finis primarius et specificus* (the fundamental and differentiating purpose) of marriage and married love.[27]

The relation between procreation-education and married love receives somewhat similar treatment in my own essay, "Source of Life".[28] Here the emphasis is on the fruitfulness of marriage, but as issuing from love: "The love-union finds its most intimate expression in the procreational act. The procreation and education are accomplished in a manner worthy of human beings, when they are the fruit and expression of love." [29] Procreation is the specifying end of marriage, distinguishing married love from all other human loves.[30] And the two, married love and procreation-education are inseparably bound as the two sides of the one coin.

The pattern of duality seeking union to issue in new life, characteristic of human sexuality and marriage, reflects in a wonderful way the union of God and his People, the union of Christ and his

[25] See footnote 11.
[26] Bernard Häring, *op. cit.*, p. 67.
[27] *Ibid.*, p. 66.
[28] "Source of Life," in *The Meaning of Christian Marriage* (see footnote 1), pp. 75–91.
[29] *Ibid.*, p. 82.
[30] *Ibid.*, pp. 85–6.

Church. And a still more sublime reality: God is love and that love as expressed in the Trinity forms the basis and pattern of married love. For the Father is not the Son and from this duality in the one divine nature the Holy Spirit issues as the fruit of their love.[31]

In laying the foundation of a satisfying theology of sex and marriage, the second approach has obvious advantages, drawing as it does on the human and divine realities that form the basis of legal rights and obligations. Perhaps its greatest practical achievement is to have reintegrated sex and marriage with love. The rediscovery of love as the center of divine and human life finds a specific application in sexual and married love. The reaction of some theologians to attempts to divorce sex and marriage from life-giving, however justified it might be, lost a good deal of its persuasive power in the face of their tolerance of the centuries-old manual dichotomy between sex, marriage and love.[32] To give love its due place in Christian marriage, the legal framework and the "essential" but "essentially subordinate" end do not suffice. It is as a community based on love (specifically sexual love) and so designed by God for new life that marriage reveals its human and divine riches and forms the basis of rights and obligations.

THE LAY CONTRIBUTION

By returning to the revealed and created sources, theology has achieved a better understanding of marriage. In this, the relation between love and life is emphasized. However, a great deal of work remains to be done at the existential level before a really satisfactory and persuasive theology of marriage appears. For too long, celibate theologians have carried on (or been left to carry on) alone in trying to interpret how God is calling man through sex and marriage. The recent crisis in Britain and the United States on contraception has shown how far communications had broken down and how remote the theologians' writing had become from

[31] *Ibid.*, p. 85.
[32] Cf. von Hildebrand, *op. cit.*, p. 83.

the daily lived experience of most Christian couples. It is only when a real exchange between the trained theologian and the articulate married couple has taken place within the confines of the Church,[33] that one can expect a theology that will be not only biblical and sacramental, emphasizing the divine realities of love and creativity, but also meaningful and helpful to the couple, by incorporating a phenomenology of sex and married life that is now woefully lacking.

A useful beginning in such exchange has already been made. The writings of Dr. John Marshall[34] have shown how to combine sound theology and medicine at a popular level in a way that carries the conviction of experience. The works of the late Reginald Trevett, *Sex and the Christian*,[35] *The Tree of Life*,[36] indicate a seeking after this kind of theology of sex.

The most organized cooperative attempts have come from the United States. Quite a useful one is *The Problem of Population: Moral and Theological Considerations*.[37] It contains the papers of a conference held at Notre Dame University in September, 1963. Two of the papers were contributed by laymen, a very thoughtful one by John E. Dunsford, "Birth Control, Abortion, Sterilization and Public Policy" on the peculiar problems posed in the United States, and one by Frederick J. Crosson, "Natural Law and Contraception". However, many other laymen are listed as participants at the conference.

A further example of such cooperation is the special issue of *Commonweal* on "Responsible Parenthood".[38] And more recently, the laity have published several valuable contributions to the growing dialogue. The first of these, edited by Michael Novak, *The*

[33] For guidance on such a dialogue, cf. R. McCormick, S.J., "Toward a Dialogue," in *Commonweal* (New York, June 5, 1964).

[34] Cf. John Marshall, *Preparing for Marriage* (London: Darton, Longman & Todd, 1962); *idem, The Infertile Period* (London: Darton, Longman & Todd, 1963); *idem*, "Family Planning: The Catholic View," in *World Justice* 3/4 (1961–62).

[35] London: Burns & Oates, 1960.

[36] London: Geoffrey Chapman, 1963.

[37] D. Barrett (ed.) (Notre Dame, 1964).

[38] See footnotes 6 and 33.

Experience of Marriage,[39] has much rewarding and revealing writing by "thirteen intelligent, articulate and committed Catholic couples" on the married life. *What Modern Catholics Think About Birth Control*, edited by William Birmingham,[40] with essays by fifteen lay Catholics, men and women, casts its net far wider than the title suggests and includes some keen philosophical and theological arguments in addition to the immediate witness of experience. The articles in *Contraception and Holiness*[41] by such laymen as Leslie Dewart on "*Casti Connubii* and the Development of Dogma" are of first importance. The witness of Anne Biezanek,[42] "the only Roman Catholic doctor in the world to run a family-planning clinic" should be received by theologians with compassion, despite some of its bizarre theology.

Two other important works by laymen deal with the particular problem of contraception and are not simply bearing witness to experience. One of these *The Time Has Come*[43] by John Rock, M.D., precipitated in some ways the present controversy, by claiming that the anovulant pill was not opposed to natural law. The other, *Contraception and Catholics*[44] by Louis Dupré is an analysis of the present arguments from authority and reason for the condemnation of contraception. Neither argument is so far definitive, he claims.

However, much of the works by laymen consisted of articles and letters in a hundred reviews and papers. L. Pyle has done a service to many of these writers and to the continuance of the dialogue in assembling so many of these sources together with more official and professional contributions in *The Pill*[45] For English and Amer-

---

[39] London: Darton, Longman & Todd, 1964.

[40] New York: Signet Books, 1964.

[41] Thomas D. Roberts, S.J. *et al.*, *Contraception and Holiness* (New York: Herder and Herder, 1964).

[42] Anne Biezanek, *All Things New* (Derby: Peter Smith, 1964).

[43] John Rock, *The Time Has Come* (New York: Knopf, 1963).

[44] Louis Dupré, *Contraception and Catholics: A New Appraisal* (Baltimore: Helicon, 1964). This includes two articles previously published: "A Re-examination of the Catholic Position on Birth Control," in *Cross Currents* 14 (1964), pp. 63ff. and "From Augustine to Janssens," in *Commonweal* (June 5, 1964), pp. 336ff.

[45] See footnote 24.

ican readers this provides a valuable source book for at least one side of the argument.

RESPONSIBLE PARENTHOOD[46]

After considerable hesitancy, theologians now speak confidently of responsible parenthood and the need to plan one's family. The biggest family physically possible is now explicitly ruled out as the ideal. Attention to the second half of the primary or specific purpose, education, might have revealed this earlier. It is not for the physically delivered infant but for the mature adult Christian, capable of taking his own place in Church and civil society, that the parents accept responsibility in marriage.

However, publicity about population problems, the awareness of the (too) great demands that a large family makes on many parents today and the development of an acceptable technique of birth regulation have led most theologians to approve responsibility in parenthood as in other human endeavors and to encourage spacing and even limiting the number of children. What the limit should be, depends on all the circumstances of the particular family, their spiritual, emotional, physical and material resources. Their ideal should be the number of children that they prayerfully believe before God they can bear and educate in a worthy human and Christian fashion.

Although children are the natural God-given result of marriage, and a married couple may not deliberately avoid them altogether without some sufficient reason,[47] there is no particular number that can be laid down for any one class or region. The conclusion seems unwarranted that because the duty to procreate is conditioned by the population needs of the day, a family of four children in the

[46] R. McCormick, S.J., "Family Size, Rhythm and the Pill," in *The Problem of Population* (Notre Dame, 1964), p. 56; John L. Thomas, "Marriage and Sexuality," in *loc. cit.*, p. 56; Denis O'Callaghan, "Family Regulations: The Catholic View," in *Irish Theological Quarterly* 30 (1963), pp. 163ff.; Bernard Häring, "Responsible Parenthood," in *loc. cit.;* M. B. Crowe and P. C. Jennings, *The Catholic Concept of Family Planning* (to be published shortly).

[47] Ford and Kelly, *op. cit.*, pp. 400ff.

United States would be sufficient to satisfy a couple's procreative duty there.[48] The population needs of their area are only one factor influencing the couple's decision and perhaps frequently the least important. The attempt to create such a standard and allow for variation through excusing causes will seem unreal to many people.

THE MEANS TO RESPONSIBLE PARENTHOOD

Abstinence

With the acceptance of responsible parenthood as a Catholic ideal, the one universally acceptable method has proved to be periodic abstinence during the fertile part of the woman's cycle. Since Pius XII's statement in 1951,[49] the theological attitude toward the use of the infertile period has developed from cautious acceptance, through presumption of reasons, to its recommendation before marriage as part of responsible married living. Provided the motive is correct, the overall good of the family, this method practiced by mutual consent and without danger of incontinence is given unqualified approval.

The only difficulty raised now about the infertile period concerns its efficiency. Most of the couples writing in *The Experience of Marriage*[50] claim to have tried seriously without real success. And this cry is repeated throughout so much of the literature in the present controversy. Yet, some of those who have most experience with it with people of all classes, like Dr. John Marshall and other doctors of the Catholic Marriage Advisory Council in Britain, claim a high rate of success with the temperature method.[51] Although the efficiency of a particular method is a medical and not a theological problem, the inability or unwillingness of many Cath-

---

[48] *Ibid.*, pp. 420ff.

[49] *Ibid.*, pp. 378–459.

[50] Only one couple, Mr. and Mrs. E., are satisfied with this method; see "No Major Problems," in *The Experience of Marriage* (footnote 1), pp. 59–67.

[51] In a hard-hitting article, "Scientific Basis of the Infertile Period," in *Catholic Herald* (Nov. 6, 1964), in which Dr. John Marshall quotes telling evidence from Palmer, a distinguished French non-Catholic gynecologist, to show the effectiveness of the method.

olic couples to use the infertile-period method has been the occasion of much theological controversy.[52]

Contraception and Sterilization

The theological consensus approving abstinence and condemning all other methods by contraception or sterilization seemed unshakable until the appearance first of an article (1961) and then a book (1963) [52a] by the eminent Catholic doctor of medicine, John Rock, claiming that the anovulant pill, in the discovery of which he played a significant role, was not contrary to nature or natural law. However eminent a doctor or well-intentioned a man, he was no theologian and the moral theologians dealt with him severely.[53]

The statement by an archbishop, however, that he had never understood the ethical argument against contraception and now had some doubts about the argument from authority, was somewhat different. And since the interview with Archbishop Roberts in *Search*, April, 1964,[54] the battle has been really joined. The condemnation of contraception (and sterilization) is defended on the basis of the Church's authoritative statements and on the basis of reason or natural law. It is necessary to review the controversy both about the argument from authority and the argument from reason.

THE CONDEMNATION OF CONTRACEPTION AND STERILIZATION

The Argument from Authority

For the defenders of the *status quo*, it is the argument from the Church's teaching authority, which is by far the most important

[52] Cf. L. Pyle, *The Pill*, passim.

[52a] John Rock, "We Can End the Battle over Birth Control," in *Good Housekeeping* (July, 1961). A condensed version appeared in *Reader's Digest* (Sept. 1961). *Idem, The Time Has Come* (New York: Knopf, 1963).

[53] John Lynch, "Notes on Moral Theology," in *Theological Studies* 23 (1962), pp. 239–43; *idem,* "The Time Has Come," in *Marriage* 45 (1963), pp. 14–17; Thomas Connolly, "The Time Has Come," in *Aust. Cath. Record* 41 (1964), pp. 12–27, 103–23.

[54] Cf. Pyle, *op. cit.*, pp. 35–90.

and the most effective. For the advocates of change it is by far the most difficult obstacle.

As usually advanced, it depends primarily on the condemnations of contraception by Pius XI in *Casti Connubii* and confirmed by Pius XII in his Address to Midwives in 1951. While most authors would agree that the formal condemnation of contraception is more solemn and precise than that of sterilization, they regard this also as clearly condemned by the Church and just as certainly immoral.[55] At any rate, it will be convenient to discuss both together.

In their reaction to recent questioning, moral theologians in almost all the English-speaking countries have reacted by declaring the present teaching of the Church irrevocable. Msgr. McReavy[56] regards the condemnation of contraception in *Casti Connubii* as "an authoritative declaration of a doctrine infallibly guaranteed by the ordinary and universal magisterium". Fr. Denis O'Callaghan regards it as unthinkable that the Church could be mistaken on this.[57] For the Americans, Frs. Ford, Kelly, Lynch, etc., the Church is irrevocably committed to the condemnation of contraception. Indeed, in their book *Marriage Questions*, Frs. Ford and Kelly regard the condemnation as at least definable doctrine and it is very likely already taught infallibly *ex jugi magisterio*.[58] On

[55] Ford and Kelly, *op. cit.*, pp. 315–18.

[56] L. L. McReavy, "Immutability of the Church's Teaching on Contraception," in *Clergy Review* 49 (1946), p. 706.

[57] Denis O'Callaghan, "Changes in Catholic Teaching," in *Irish Ecclesiastical Review* (1964), p. 402.

[58] Ford and Kelly, *op. cit.*, p. 277. Cf. J. Lynch, "Notes on Moral Theology," in *Theological Studies* 25 (1964), p. 236. The first break in the united front presented by American professors of Moral Theology, or at least Jesuit moralists, seems to be the article by Woodstock professor Felix Cardegna, S.J., "Contraception, the Pill and Responsible Parenthood," in *Theological Studies* (Dec. 1964), pp. 611–36. He adopts the position defended by Professor Janssens and expresses the hope "that the use of the pill as proposed by Janssens will be allowed by the Church, at least as a probable view among theologians and permissible in practice" (p. 636). His distinction on moral grounds between the pill and other methods does not seem, as it stands, any more convincing than that of Janssens on whom he depends. He is however aware of this and advances the discussion, particularly on sterilization.

the other side of the world in Australia, Fr. Timothy Connolly speaks of it as infallibly taught by the Church.[59]

There is less agreement on the technical dogmatic note to be assigned to the outlawing of sterilization,[60] permanent or temporary, especially by the use of anovulants. The principle of Pius XI would according to Fr. Kelly[61] also include "direct sterilization— that is, sterilization as a contraceptive measure". And Pius XII, he points out, rejected it several times as "an even more radical infringement of the moral law than contraceptive acts". The contraceptive use of the anovulant pills was explicitly condemned by Pius XII in 1958, and even if it lacks the solemnity and continuity of the condemnation of other forms of contraceptives, it is no less certainly wrong.[61a] Even Fr. Ford almost displays some slight hesitancy in regard to the irrevocable character of the condemnation of the "pill",[62] and Fr. O'Callaghan[63] believes that Paul VI's statement "suggests at most that the question of the pill" is still an open question in the sense that the teaching of Pius XII is not regarded as immutably definitive.

The hierarchy of England and Wales, however, did not indulge in any such subtle distinction in their condemnation of contraception (and contraceptive sterilization): "the plain teaching of Christ". It is no longer, they said, "an open question".[64]

That the official teaching is not irrevocable is presupposed in any Catholic attempt to change the teaching. Dr. Rock's plea for

[59] Thomas Connolly, *loc. cit.*, p. 26.

[60] See footnote 55.

[61] Gerald Kelly, S.J., "Christian Unity and Christian Marriage," in *Theology Digest* 9 (1963), p. 205.

[61a] *Ibid.*

[62] "The contraceptive pill as we have it today does not differ in any way from the pill condemned by the Holy See. No new medical factors have been made known which make its contraceptive use today morally different from the contraceptive use which Pius XII declared immoral five and a half years ago. Consequently, unless and until the Holy See gives its approval to some other teaching (a highly unlikely eventuality), no lesser authority in the Church, and least of all a private theologian is at liberty to teach a different doctrine or to free Catholics from their obligation to accept a papal teaching." Quoted from *N.C.W.C. News Service*, February 15, 1964, in L. Pyle, *op. cit.*

[63] Denis O'Callaghan, *loc. cit.*

[64] Cf. L. Pyle, *op. cit.*, p. 95.

the acceptance of the "pill" as in harmony with "nature" claimed that the teaching of Pius XII on this topic could and should be changed.[65] But a much more radical challenge was to follow. Archbishop Roberts' doubts about the argument from authority did not distinguish between the methods of birth control.[66] In the meantime, American philosopher, Louis Dupré, in a well-considered article maintained that the matter had not been infallibly and irrevocably decided, either by being solemnly defined in *Casti Connubii* or "taught unanimously and explicitly over a long period of time under the ordinary teaching of the Church". Major disagreements about solemn definition or a genuine tradition rule out infallibility.[67]

The rejection of infallibility demands, however, a more theological analysis of the situation than this. Such an analysis has been attempted by Gregory Baum, O.S.A.[68] It is necessary to distinguish between "the solemn definitions of councils and popes speaking *ex cathedra* and the ordinary magisterium of the universal Church" and other authoritative, but non-infallible teaching. In constituting the ordinary, universal magisterium he regards it necessary that the bishops arrive at agreement not through "external conformity" or as a result of "the authority of the pope" but by making their own contribution, acting as true *judices fidei* in the Christian communities entrusted to them and so attaining real internal conviction. For this, a long drawn-out process will usually be necessary.[69] The clear implication is that such a process has not taken place in regard to contraception.

However, there remains the non-infallible authoritative teaching of the Church (the highest form of it—papal encyclicals, decrees,

[65] John Rock, *The Time Has Come*, pp. 159ff.
[66] *Loc. cit.*
[67] Louis Dupré, *Catholics and Contraception* (Baltimore, 1964), p. 31, (see footnote 44).
[68] Gregory Baum, "Is the Church's Position on Birth Control Infallible?" in *The Ecumenist* 2 (1964), pp. 83–5. Reprinted with some additional material and changes as "Can the Church Change Her Position on Birth Control?" in *Contraception and Holiness* (New York: Herder and Herder, 1964), pp. 311ff. Subsequent references are to the latter (book) version.
[69] *Ibid.*, p. 314.

etc.), which demands a real internal religious assent,[70] which is not an assent of faith, however, and which allows for the theologian who has real reasons to regard the judgment as wrong or inadequate to ask to have it reviewed.[71] It is in this light that Gregory Baum sees the teaching on contraception. And he uses as an analogy the 19th-century papal statements, etc., on religious liberty and the present attitude.[72] In a stimulating article[73] that appeared after these notes were prepared, Canon F. H. Drinkwater arrives at the conclusion that contraception has not been infallibly condemned. He criticizes the "emotional exaggeration of the infallibility of the Church" which has been so common recently, and enthusiastically endorses Gregory Baum's article.

Analogies such as those of usury, religious liberty, etc., are frequently used in order to show the possibility of change or evolution in the Church's teaching on a moral matter based on deeper insight into the matter involved and a change of circumstances in which the moral teaching is to be employed. But each topic of this kind has to be examined on its own merits and the first serious attempt in English to establish the possibility of a doctrinal development that would admit *Casti Connubii* in its proper content and on its own narrow terms and at the same time allow for the use of contraceptives in our own day is that of Leslie Dewart.[74] The limitations in understanding sexuality and the place of sexual love in marriage, the confusion of *coitus interruptus* with other forms of contraception, the overriding desire to protect the traditional doctrine that marriage was for procreation, made indiscriminate condemnation of contraception by *Casti Connubii* intelligible, even excusable but no longer adequately refined for the increased understanding or present-day personal and social

[70] *Ibid.*, p. 315.
[71] *Ibid.*, p. 317.
[72] *Ibid.*, pp. 317–18.
[73] F. H. Drinkwater, "Ordinary and Universal," in *The Clergy Review* (Jan. 1965), pp. 2–22.
[74] Leslie Dewart, "*Casti Connubii* and the Development of Dogma," in *Contraception and Holiness*, pp. 202–310. A very penetrating criticism of *Contraception and Holiness* in an article review of the same by Herbert McCabe, O.P. (*New Blackfriars*, Feb. 1965) gives unqualified praise to Leslie Dewart's contribution.

needs. So a further attitude developed permitting contraceptives not to avoid children but for the overall good of the family and society and to enable the couple to develop in their Christian love of each other through its spontaneous Christian expression. Mr. Dewart's article deserves careful reading by all moral theologians.

The Argument from Scripture and Tradition[75]

Despite references to the example of Onan in official documents, exegetes and moral theologians today are very hesitant about interpreting it as a condemnation of contraception.[76] The argument from tradition is unsatisfactory also. St. Augustine seems to be the first to refer to contraception, and that on the basis of the Genesis text.[77] His ideas about sex being used without sin only for procreation and his subsequent influence make it very hard to establish a genuine tradition. The repeated condemnations by the Holy Office in the 19th century are some indication.[78]

However, the conclusion of Sullivan,[79] "that an articulated tradition condemning contraception exists prior to the last three decades appears tenuous", is a bit severe. His evidence seems incomplete, even in reporting official condemnations as beginning in 1951. There are at least two earlier ones, 1822 and 1842, recorded in Denzinger-Schönmetzer and a history of theologians' condemnation in the previous centuries.[80]

At any rate, there has been a great development in the understanding of sexuality and sexual intercourse in marriage since the time of St. Augustine and even of St. Thomas; and as we have witnessed, the emergence today of the ideas of responsible parenthood with its consequence of some birth limitation and perfection through sexual love, it is impossible to say that the evolution is

[75] Cf. Ford and Kelly, op. cit., pp. 235ff.; Louis Dupré, op. cit., pp. 17–27; Dan Sullivan, "A History of Catholic Thinking on Contraception," in What Modern Catholics Think About Birth Control, W. Birmingham (ed.), pp. 28–72.

[76] Louis Dupré, op. cit., pp. 17–19, quotes A. M. Dubarle, O.P., in favor of this.

[77] Ibid.

[78] Denzinger-Schönmetzer, Enchiridion Symbolorum (Freiburg, 1963).

[79] Dan Sullivan, op. cit., p. 65.

[80] Louis Dupré, op. cit., pp. 32–34.

complete or that there is a compelling argument from early tradition outlawing contraception.

The Argument from Reason and Natural Law

The arguments from reason or natural law[81] reduce to three types: (a) that based on the inviolability of the generative process; (b) a personalist argument from the nature of married love; (c) an argument from the consequences of the contrary.

The first type of argument[82] is usually some variation or explanation of Pius XI's statement that "since the conjugal act is designed of its very nature for the generation of children, those who, in performing it deliberately deprive it of its natural power and capacity, act against nature and commit a deed that is shameful and immoral". As Fr. Gerald Kelly states: "God has written a certain definite plan into the conjugal act and man's freedom to change it is at most limited to accidentals—contraception is an attack on the invisible divine plan for the beginning of human life." [83] This argument would also include direct or contraceptive sterilization, permanent or temporary as contrary to the divine purpose of the sexual function in suppressing the procreative power.[84]

The peculiar character of this faculty and act is derived from its

---

[81] Several articles have appeared recently dealing with the idea of "natural law" as background to discussion on contraception. In general, they have insisted on the personalist element of natural moral law. It is not determined simply by physiological data, they have also stressed the dynamic or evolutionary aspect of it, particularly in the relation between sexual activity and conservation of the race. Cf. F. J. Crossan, "Natural Law and Contraception," Barrett (ed.) *The Problem of Population* (Notre Dame, 1964), pp. 113–31; Louis Dupré, "Natural End and Natural Law," in *Catholics and Contraception*, pp. 37–52; Frederick E. Flynn, "Natural Law and Overpopulation," in *What Modern Catholics Think About Birth Control*, W. Birmingham (ed.), pp. 164–73; Martin Redfern, "Natural Law or Supernatural Order," in *Slant* 1/3 (1964), pp. 6–11. The usual arguments from natural law are given in the text, but they do not normally involve any questioning of the meaning or relevance of natural law.

[82] Cf. Ford and Kelly, "Why the Church Rejects Contraception," *op. cit.*, pp. 279–314.

[83] Gerald Kelly, S.J., "Contraception and Natural Law," in *Proceedings of the Convention of the Catholic Theological Society of America 1963* (New York, 1963), pp. 28–31.

[84] Cf. Ford and Kelly, *op. cit.*, pp. 318ff.

social function, given as it is not for man's personal benefit but for the preservation of the race, the "good of the species".[85] The stewardship that man has of his body and that allows him to subordinate directly any other part of the body to the good of the whole is limited in this sphere by the social purpose or good of sex, which is superior to the individual good.

The argument is developed in other terms by speaking of contraception as a *frustration* of the sexual faculty, divorcing it from its inherent purpose, or *finis operis* in generation. The same idea is present in speaking of contraception as opposed to the primary or at least an essential purpose of the conjugal act. Or in speaking of contraception as involving an inherent contradiction "in willing an act whose primary natural purpose is the procreation of children and at the same time willing another act to prevent this purpose being fulfilled".[86]

These arguments (really variations on the one argument) have been severely criticized during the last year or so. To say that "the conjugal act is designed of its nature for the generation of children" and so may never be divorced from this purpose from one point of view proves too much,[87] as it would exclude intercourse of sterile couples, after menopause and during the infertile period. Interpreting it as meaning the act must remain potentially generative even though *per accidens* generation is impossible, makes little sense according to these critics. The woman's fertile days by nature itself are no more than five in the month, and to speak of the deliberate choice of the infertile days and deliberate exclusion of the possibility of generation as consistent with placing a potentially procreative act has its own difficulties. All it can mean, in the mind of one critic, is that a particular biological or physiological pattern is followed and this is not of obvious moral value.[88]

A more interesting line of criticism accepts the inherent finality

[85] Cf. Denis O'Callaghan, "Fertility Control by Medication," in *Irish Theological Quarterly* 27 (1960), p. 8.

[86] J. J. Farraher, S.J., "Notes on Moral Theology," in *Theological Studies* 21 (1960), p. 601. For a summary of, and some critical comments on, these arguments, cf. Kelly, *op. cit.*, pp. 36–42.

[87] "Extract from a Longer Work," in *Slant* 1/3 (1964), pp. 15f.

[88] *Ibid.*

of sexual activity as designed for procreation, but from this it is possible to deduce that one may not use sex in marriage and exclude children, but not that every sexual act must result in or be liable to result in generation.[89] Indeed, the attainment of the complete specific or primary end of marriage and sexual activity, the procreation *and education* of children will frequently demand postponement or avoidance of further pregnancy.[90]

The admission of exceptional uses of the "pill",[91] which are not simply therapeutic, *e.g.*, in danger of rape, to regularize the cycle (and so make the infertile period secure and so avoid children) to extend the alleged infertility during lactation, for psychological reasons[92] have evoked further criticisms.[93] Can the suppression of ovulation by the "pill" to avoid conception be intrinsically immoral in other circumstances such as danger to the wife's health or the existing children or the mutual love of the couple, if it is conceded to be moral in these?

The way natural law is used suggests to some people that the good of the whole person is being subjected to a biological or physiological process. And the appeal for the need to conserve the race makes little impression in an age in which the problem is overpopulation not underpopulation. Perhaps as one writer points out, the stage has come when the mutual love aspect exceeds in urgency and importance the procreative aspect, so that while responsible procreation is maintained when generation is not desirable, the sexual expression of love may be achieved by the use of contraceptives.[94]

[89] Herbert McCabe, "Contraceptives and Natural Law," in *New Blackfriars* 46 (1964), pp. 89ff. John L. Thomas, S.J., *loc. cit.*, p. 49: "It would appear more in keeping with the presently known facts to maintain that not the individual act of intercourse but what might be called the *process of sexual relations* is procreative."

[90] This may be admitted by defenders of the *status quo* also, but they would only allow abstinence, periodic or complete as a solution.

[91] Cf. Ford and Kelly, *op. cit.*, pp. 345ff.; John Lynch, *op. cit.*, pp. 239–47; Denis O'Callaghan, *op. cit.*, pp. 9ff.

[92] No theologian writing in English approves this, as far as I know, but some Europeans are cited as approving it. Cf. Louis Dupré, *op. cit.*, p. 35, where he quotes P. Anciaux.

[93] *Ibid.*

[94] Cf. Michael Novak, "Toward a Positive Sexual Morality," Birmingham (ed.), *op. cit.*, p. 110.

Not all these arguments are of equal weight. Many of them have been considered by theologians before and rejected. The "non-therapeutic" uses for example mentioned above are not conceded by all theologians. And it is possible to distinguish the employment of a contraceptive in a voluntary act of intercourse in marriage and its employment in an involuntary violent act. However, the argument from the finality of sexual activity applies more obviously to the series of acts and the total married life than to the individual act of sexual intercourse.

Personalist Arguments

Here an attempt is made to analyze married love and to show that the proper and full sexual expression of that love excludes contraceptives. Dietrich von Hildebrand[95] regards contraception as a desecration of this love and an act of irreverence to God, but basically by violating his design for expressing married love. To my mind, the deliberate divorce of this sexual expression of love from its "openness to life" reduces what should be mutual giving to mutual possessing and so destroys true married love.[96]

In a long article entitled "Contraception and Conjugal Love", Paul Quay, S.J., analyzes the phenomenology of human sexuality and sexual love and concludes that "the woman who uses a diaphragm has closed herself to her husband. She has accepted his affection but not his substance—such mates perform what appears to be the act of love but is only a sham; they abuse the symbol of the gift of one's self to another until it betokens precisely the withholding of this gift".[97] This falsifying of the conjugal act through contraception in preventing it from being an expression and symbol of each partner's total gift of self to the other is used by many other theologians, for example, Ford,[98] Kelly[99] and Duhamel.[100] For them to be a true act of love it must be "an act of procreative love".

[95] Von Hildebrand, *op. cit.*, p. 96.
[96] Enda McDonagh, *op. cit.*, p. 84.
[97] In *Theological Studies* 22 (1961), pp. 18–40, especially pp. 35f.
[98] Ford and Kelly, *op. cit.*, pp. 289–91.
[99] Gerald Kelly, S.J., *op. cit.*, pp. 40–42.
[100] G. Duhamel, S.J., *The Catholic Church and Birth Control* (New York, 1963), pp. 13–14.

Dupré[101] criticizes this argument on the grounds that man, as an historical creature, cannot commit himself fully in any one act. This is true in the sense that he cannot commit or express himself exhaustively and definitively, but he can commit himself totally as he now is. Otherwise, the permanent commitment of marriage could not be undertaken through one act of consent, or the acceptance of God in faith or rejection of him in serious sin would be impossible for man to accomplish in any one act. However, the argument has a certain *ad hoc* air, elaborated because one already knows that contraception is wrong. Further reflection on sexual love and its expression is necessary before it could be regarded as entirely convincing. Yet, if there is a single argument that would be effective against the individual contraceptive act, the best hope of finding it seems to be in an analysis of the conjugal act as a communication of conjugal love.

Argument from the Consequences of Accepting Contraception

The consequences considered here have nothing to do with difficulties about the Church's teaching authority, the embarrassment of theologians or the confusion and resentment of a large part of the faithful, if such a change should take place. Some of these are serious consequences but, except for the teaching authority already considered, of no theological value.

Although one still finds it mentioned occasionally, very little serious argument has been based on the physical and psychological harm of contraceptives.[102] In fact, some recent Catholic lay writing has tended to stress the physical and psychological damage caused by their nonuse,[103] through the inefficiency of the infertile-period (rhythm) method or the nervous tension caused by abstinence.

The social consequences of contraception have always been stressed in Catholic writing. The disappearance of the race argument is hard to take seriously nowadays, but the other social evils

[101] Louis Dupré, *op. cit.*, pp. 77f.
[102] McHugh & Callan, *Moral Theology 11* (New York, 1958), p. 615.
[103] Cf. *The Experience of Marriage*, Michael Novak (ed.), (New York, 1964), *passim*.

of what Fr. de Lestapis has called "the contraceptive civilization" have received some attention. Some aspects of this are suggested by Fr. Zimmermann, S.V.D. in the *American Ecclesiastical Review*, where he lists some of the results of the Eugenics Protection Law, 1948, in Japan, permitting the sale of contraceptives. "Abortions have multiplied . . . [there is] a strong desire to avoid babies—a general indifference toward self discipline in sexual behavior" as a result of "the promotion of contraception".[104]

Here some possible theological consequences of the permission of contraception have to be considered. Dr. Rock's attempt to have the "pill" approved, while other contraceptives remain outlawed, did not get much support. His argument that the "pill" supplies for or assists nature, while leaving the conjugal act intact, was not accepted as convincing.[105] The diaphragm, douche and spermatocidal jelly also leave the act intact and with far less disturbance to the generative system. Between one automatic way of excluding conception and another, at least where the conjugal act is properly performed, no clear moral distinction has emerged.[106] And would it prove increasingly difficult to outlaw the condom as a barrier to complete physical contact or perhaps *coitus interruptus*, where no other method was available, and the need was pressing, once you admit any form of contraception?

Various forms of sterilization could perhaps, as Archbishop Roberts implies, be justified in extreme cases like India.[107] And must one stop there? Once you divorce the love from life-giving, why not sodomy? contraceptive fornication as an expression of love and even homosexual acts, so long as they expressed love? This argument was developed by Bishop Gore of the Church of England in his opposition to the spread of birth control and more recently in a report submitted by a minority group of Anglicans

[104] A. Zimmermann, S.V.D., "Some Reasons Why the Church Opposes Contraception," in *American Ecclesiastical Review* 150 (1964), pp. 254–55.
[105] John Rock, *op. cit.*
[106] Louis Dupré, *op. cit.*
[107] T. Roberts, "Contraception and War," in *Objections to Roman Catholicism* (New York: Lippincott), p. 173; *idem*, "Introduction," in *Contraception and Holiness*, p. 20.

to the bishops at the 1958 Lambeth Conference. It is frequently endorsed by Catholics.[108] How far it is cogent, is not clear.

In an interesting attempt to develop "positive sexual morality" Michael Novak[109] is content that he can uphold the act of intercourse as "physically symbolizing" the permanent love-union of the partners and as "apt for generation" when what he calls "the biological imperative", the obligation of the couple to have a child, so commands. Intercourse belongs to marriage and "is for the preservation of the race. But not every act of intercourse". The various perversions can be excluded as violating one or other aspect of his definition of intercourse.

CONCLUSION

The controversy is far from complete. By the time these notes appear some critical development may have taken place. Despite the confusion in one particular area, real advances have been made toward a fully integrated theology of marriage. The cooperation of committed and articulate Catholic lay people promises to provide theological understanding of sexuality and marriage in action that was not possible before our time. The difficulties about contraception should not blind one to the progress made or the possibilities for good inherent in the debate. As yet no clear convincing argument from observation and reason has emerged on the authoritative side (or on the other for that matter). Perhaps no single argument is possible, and what one should look for is a convergence of arguments from revelation and reason, from philosophy, scientific observation and personal experience—all welded together under the guidance of the Holy Spirit to provide the Church with a further decisive illumination.

[108] Cf. Ford and Kelly, *op. cit.*, pp. 291f.; Gerald Kelly, S.J., "Contraception and Natural Law," *op. cit.*, pp. 34–5.

[109] Michael Novak, "Toward a Positive Sexual Morality," *loc. cit.*, pp. 113f.

PART III

DO-C DOCUMENTATION

CONCILIUM

DIRECTOR: Leo Alting von Geusau
Groningen, Netherlands

ASS'T DIRECTOR: M.-J. Le Guillou, O.P.
Boulogne-sur-Seine, France

✠ Giacomo Cardinal Lercaro / *Bologna, Italy*

The Decree on Ecumenism and the Dialogue with non-Catholic Eastern Churches

At a Congress held at Beirut during the spring of this year I had an opportunity to explain what I thought about the ecumenical importance of the Constitution on the Liturgy. I am now glad to accept the kind and pressing invitation, extended to me by the Rector of the Collegio Greco, to speak on the Decree on Ecumenism insofar as it affects the dialogue between the Catholic Church and the non-Catholic Churches of the Middle East.

At first I hesitated to undertake such a difficult and "specialized" subject in such a well-informed milieu, being a Westerner myself. This hesitation was overcome by the profound conviction that, together with the Constitution on the Church and the Constitution on the Sacred Liturgy, the Decree on Ecumenism forms an indivisible trilogy because, in contrast with other schemata on which the Council is engaged, these three deal directly with the most profound aspects of the Church. All the other decrees that the Council may promulgate are necessarily connected in one way or another with these three texts which may be considered as the core of the Council's task according to John XXIII's wishes.

* Address given by His Eminence Giacomo Cardinal Lercaro, Archbishop of Bologna, at the Collegio Greco, in Rome, on Wednesday, November 11, 1964.

With the Decree on Ecumenism the Council means to lay the foundation, from the Catholic point of view, of that dialogue between Christians of which Pope Paul VI has developed certain particularly important aspects in his encyclical *Ecclesiam Suam* and in his opening address for the third session of the Council. In this address (September 14, 1964), the Pope gave a kind of solemn pledge to the Churches and Communities represented by non-Catholic observers: "Moreover, mindful of the fact that the same apostle entreated us to preserve the unity of the spirit through the bond of peace, because there is but one Lord, one faith, one baptism, one God and Father of all, we shall attempt, in loyalty to the oneness of Christ's Church, to understand better and to accept all that is authentic and acceptable in the various Christian denominations that are separated from us." This, then, was the line he wished the Council to pursue in order to prepare the way for what he himself called the "reconstitution of unity". The dialogue with the brethren not yet in full communion with us, mentioned in *Ecclesiam Suam*, was therefore explained, insofar as Catholics are concerned, as the great pursuit of the unity that had to be found again. It does not only consist in presenting others with a truth, already possessed by us in a way that is accessible to them, but, above all, in getting to know them and in accepting the genuine riches that is theirs: an attempt at comprehension and assimilation from within. And it was really with this end in view that the Decree on Ecumenism was prepared, drawn up and finally approved by the Council.

It might be useful here to make a preliminary observation. The Decree on Ecumenism is not a conciliar *constitution* but a *decree*. This does not limit its importance among the acts of the Council. It simply means that the text contains pastoral implications and things to be put into practice at once. Anyone can see that it contains the essential elements of a Catholic theology of ecumenism, as well as principles by which Catholic activity should be guided toward Christian unity. Its very first, rather extensive paragraph after the preamble gives us a doctrinal synthesis on the unity and singleness of the Church, based principally on the theology of the eucharist as it has been proposed in a new light by the Constitution on the Liturgy and the Constitution on the Church, each in its own way. The mystery of the Church, being the expression of that divine love which, in its design for salvation, wants to bring all men together, is not only intimately linked with Christ's great sacerdotal prayer after the last supper (John 17), but it is also essentially connected with the saving acts of Christ and their continuation in the Church's mission: the eucharist and the cross, the promise and sending of the Spirit after the resurrection, and the mission of the apostles so that the world may believe. Nothing else in the birth, growth and life of the Church until the return of Christ in glory has meaning except in relation to that mystery of the exaltation of Christ, constituted Lord at the right hand of the Father, and leaving us the Paraclete as pledge of the final reconciliation he has brought about between the Father who sent him and that dispersed humanity which he had to bring together again.

The unity of the Church, *i.e.*, the unity of Christians among themselves in communion with the Lord and inhabited by the same divine Spirit, is but an image, an efficacious symbol of the unity of the divine Persons in the blessed Trinity. This is an aspect of the Christian faith, which is dear to traditional theology and finds a living expression in the heritage of the Eastern Churches, as will be developed later on.

The Decree on Ecumenism has, therefore, a sound theological foundation which faithful and clergy should constantly meditate on if they wish to see the work of reconstituting the unity, willed by the Lord himself, in its true perspective. This theological basis which, at the request of many Fathers of the Council, emphasizes the role played by the Holy Spirit more strongly than was done in the first draft, in no way neglects the institutional aspect of the Church's structure. But the structure of the divinely instituted ministry has been put back there in its functional framework, and this fills the best pages of the Constitution on the Church, insofar as the ecumenical dialogue is concerned. There, the Church clearly appears as the mystery of salvation and as the People of God on its way toward the kingdom, and there, the various ministries find their full application: the three functions of teaching, government and, above all, sanctification have been entrusted by Christ to the College of the twelve apostles so that the Church can spread throughout the world till the consummation of the present age, that is, till the return of the Lord of glory. Among those "Twelve", Peter and his successors occupy a special place, and the text clearly shows that their function of confirming in the faith and of tending Christ's flock in unity is, above all, a ministry of love: to maintain unity in the flock through the bond of love which is the new command by which Christ's disciples are recognized. But the text of the decree has most aptly reminded us in a discreet but definite way that, however essential these ministries are to the Church, they are only functional because ultimately the only reason for their existence is the service of the Church on her pilgrimage, and in the end only Jesus Christ himself will remain, who is the cornerstone of the whole building and the true shepherd of our souls.

Having clearly laid down these premises, the decree can proceed with the practical consequences of this theology of Christian unity and establish the principles of a sound ecumenism.

The different parts of the decree have each their own importance, but I shall now concentrate particularly on the part which the Council has devoted to the non-Catholic Eastern Churches. Everyone knows that Pope Paul has set the example of this special and outstanding interest in the Orthodox Churches by various gestures he has made in this respect.

The meeting with the Ecumenical Patriarch at Jerusalem, the restitution of the head of St. Andrew to the Church of Patras, the message he has sent to the Rhodes Conference—all this shows that a great step forward has been made under the influence of the Spirit. These gestures and many others of lesser importance but equally revealing are indications that a new era has been opened in the relations between the Catholic Church and the Eastern Churches which we considered for centuries as separated Churches.

But these symbolic gestures would be meaningless if this attitude were not adopted by the whole Catholic Church, both leaders and faithful. Here the Church must first clearly indicate by the decisions of the Council what starting points are indispensable for a dialogue that may one day lead to the reconstitution of unity.

This is the keynote of Chapter III of the decree, which wants to throw into relief the characteristic features of those Churches with whom we wish to establish a dialogue.

This part of the decree sets out three basic principles:

1. In spite of their separation, the Eastern Communities have remained Churches.

2. These Eastern Churches possess a heritage of their own that justifies their particularism in matters of liturgy, spirituality, canon law and even theology.

3. Catholics must begin by respecting and loving that heritage and those particularities of the Eastern Churches so that these may have their legitimate place within the reconstituted unity.

I

THE ORTHODOX CHURCHES HAVE REMAINED CHURCHES

We must first note that, since the rupture in the 11th century, a continuous tradition of pontifical documents has given them the name of Eastern Churches in spite of the fact that they were no longer in communion with the See of Rome. The fact that this was not a matter of an occasional mark of goodwill but of a usage which continued practically without a break till our own time, shows that we are dealing here with an undeniable ecclesiological value. This fact must be explained so that we can draw consequences which will lead us to a more realistic view of what these Orthodox Churches are in themselves and in relation to the Catholic Church.

The first task of those who had to draw up the first part of the decree was to place the Eastern Churches in their true historical context. The great temptation of Catholic ecclesiology during these last centuries has been to start with an abstract attitude toward things, based on purely logical arguments rooted in a point of view that was correct in itself but one-sided; and it was often difficult to escape completely from this temptation. The very fact that many Catholic theologians had lost contact with the historical reality of the Christian East since the Middle Ages caused them to work out ecclesiological syntheses in which certain aspects of the ecclesial mystery were overstressed while others, not less important, were more or less lost sight of. In its particular approach to the Eastern Churches, therefore, the decree aims first of all at a return to a fairer perspective based on history and which made it possible to account for the ecclesial character that the Eastern Orthodox Churches have preserved up to the present day.

To establish this historical fact is simple enough, but it is often difficult for a present-day Catholic theologian to understand the full implications of this fact. While in the Christian West, the Latin world, there was only one Church, that of Rome, which was undoubtedly of apostolic origin, there were several Churches in the East, the cradle of Christianity, which could legitimately claim an apostolic foundation. Think, for instance, of Jerusalem, Antioch, Thessalonica and Cyprus. As these Churches developed, several rapidly assumed a character of their own and became the great historical patriarchates. To these was added, in the course of the 4th century, the Church of Constantinople which soon took first place among the old Sees of the East because of the political importance of the city, Constantinople having become the capital of the Eastern Empire and the New Rome of the Emperors. One can argue about the legitimacy of the claim of Constantinople to the primacy of the East, but the fact remains: when once the primacy of Constantinople after Rome had been recognized and sanctioned by the East, it was because of ecclesiological considerations very different from those of Rome. The unique and privileged apostolicity of Rome in the West made it possible for the Latins very soon to recognize its exceptional role and its primacy. In contrast, the East put a special emphasis on the fraternal relations which should prevail among Churches, each of which could claim an equally venerable apostolic foundation.

This is the point of the rather long addition to paragraph 23 of the new draft of Chapter III in the Constitution on the Church. Some Churches have been "matrices of the faith", as Tertullian says, because of their apostolic origin. They gave birth to other Churches that grouped themselves round the Mother Church quite naturally. They were linked by bonds of communion in faith and charity, and became Sister Churches, each of which had her own theological, spiritual, liturgical and disciplinary heritage. Now, the Constitution on the Church recognized this historical fact when it dealt with the relations among the bishops within the College of bishops. And so the Decree on Ecumenism was bound to underline this vigorously, because this fact lies at the root of Orthodox ecclesiology. For this is the way in which the Eastern Churches understand their own past and explain their present situation. The bonds linking them together are above all the bonds of fraternal love and communion, based on a common faith and sacramental life. And it should be noted *en passant:* if one reflects on God's design for his Church, one can but marvel at the fact that in spite of the absence of centralization (because of the rejection of Rome's primacy) the Eastern Churches, whether derived from Byzantium for the last one thousand years or from the non-Chalcedonian Churches of Egypt and Syria for fifteen centuries, have preserved intact the essentials of the apostolic faith and of the ecclesial structure.

This fact should make it clear for us that this is not merely a matter of a mysterious intervention of divine providence by which each of the faithful as an individual can receive the sacraments for his salvation because his community, though separated from Rome, has preserved the validity of the sacraments. This individualistic outlook, which explains things too glibly by referring to the "good faith" of the non-Catholic Easterner, should be definitely recognized today as inadequate. It is not merely a matter of providence caring for individuals in its own hidden fashion. The problem lies on a very different level. Apart from a few doctrinal points, defined by the Catholic Church after the separation, the whole membership of the Eastern Churches has remained substantially intact.

It is not enough to point to the settled conservatism of the East as an argument, as is done too often. No; we are here confronted with a factual situation where the Eastern Churches not only have a validly consecrated hierarchy—a point never questioned by Catholic theology—but also a sacramental and liturgical life identical with our own as well as a body of doctrine that firmly maintains truths defined by the Ecumenical Councils common to both East and West, and so we are forced to look beyond a mere individualistic interpretation. The problem does no longer lie simply in the validity of the sacraments and their efficacy for the members of non-Roman Communities: it lies on the much deeper level of ecclesiology.

If the celebration of the eucharist by the ecclesial Community gathered round its bishop is the basis of all sound ecclesiology, as both the Constitution on the Liturgy and the Constitution on the Church affirm, we have to reexamine the whole approach, common among many theologians since the Counter-Reformation. We must get beyond the purely juridical approach and courageously look at the root of the matter. Although there is no full communion between Rome and the non-Catholic East, these Eastern Churches have genuinely preserved the character of Church in the bonds of apostolic faith and sacramental communion. We have here communities that have preserved the essential marks of ecclesial reality. This is why the Catholic Church has always treated them as Churches, as I mentioned before.

Here I must say at once that the text of the decree, thanks to the amendments proposed by many of the Fathers, shows particular courage in the first part of paragraph 15 by taking a line which will appear audacious to many. Indeed, it clearly affirms that the celebration of the eucharist in each of these Churches really "builds up" the one holy Church as a whole, and contributes to her growth. It goes further. The concelebration of their priests with their bishop or of different local bishops together manifests their "communion". Because of the sacramental reality that links them together and the uninterrupted succession of their bishops from the apostles on, in a faith substantially the same as ours, this "communion" cannot be anything else but an authentic participation in the Communion of the true Church of Christ.

Once we have frankly accepted the authentic ecclesial nature of the Eastern Churches, there remains an obvious difficulty. The Orthodox Churches reject the Roman doctrine of the primacy and infallibility of Peter's successor as defined by Vatican I. In order to avoid illusions we should recognize at once that this is not a false problem or a simple misunderstanding easily disposed of by honest research and understanding of the facts of history. No, this is the heart of the problem. In order to look at it objectively we must turn our attention again to the data of Eastern ecclesiology such as they are incorporated in history from the very beginning, as mentioned above. On this point the difference in perspective between Catholics and Orthodox has its roots in an ecclesiology that has been lived differently by both sides and has developed on different lines in the course of centuries. As a Communion of Sister Churches of apostolic origin founded on fraternal union in faith and love, the Eastern Churches have never felt explicitly the need for the Roman primacy in the same way as the Western Church. It is not that, during the centuries before the break, they did not recognize, at least implicitly, the exceptional role of the Church of Rome, particularly when difficulties arose in matters of faith which in the last resort had to be decided. Historical evidence, not abundant in quantity but definite enough, clearly shows that communion with the bishop of Rome was for them the touchstone of orthodoxy and unity in the one Church of Christ. The decree recognizes this fairly.

But this conception of the role of the Church of Rome fell within the framework of that ecclesiology of a Communion of Sister Churches. The whole life of the Church was and still is felt and lived there within the concept of a local Church of which the bishop is the head and which finds its most perfect expression in the celebration of the eucharist with the bishop.

Beyond this horizon of the local Church, the relations with the other Churches are thought of, first of all, as a Communion within the patriarchal synod that groups the Daughter Churches around the *matrix fidei*, the patriarchal See from which they have sprung. There they maintain that communion among themselves and live their ecclesial life in the communion of faith brought about by the same love of Christ, expressed in a common sacramental life.

The Patriarchs, in turn, are united among themselves by the bond of mutual communion of which the synodal letters give the most tangible and the most moving proof since the earliest times, and even since the apostolic age. One has but to think of the letters of St. Paul and those of Ignatius of Antioch to see that these are striking evidence of the role these epistolary exchanges played in maintaining the unity of faith and the bond of peace in the love of Christ. But with the exception of the Ecumenical Councils which, as we know, were only sporadic and occasional manifestations of the collegial communion of the universal Church in the eyes of the Christian East, each patriarchal Church, and within each patriarchate every local Church, lived an essentially autonomous life from the point of view of discipline, liturgy, spirituality and theology. It is hardly surprising that this attitude, justified by an ecclesiology hailing from the days of the apostles, did not encourage a doctrinal development such as took place in the West where it was always pivoted on the See of Rome.

This difference in ecclesiological perspective has caused growing misunderstandings between the East and Rome, and under the pressure of historical circumstances the East gradually lost the sense of the need for communion with the See of Rome within the universal Church. It had never felt this need as we did. When the West tended increasingly toward the explicit recognition of the Christ-willed privileges of Peter's successor, the East did not follow that road. Two ecclesiologies, which ought to complement each other and the importance of which we are beginning to rediscover, hardened and became mutually resented as incompatible and even contradictory. And yet, the East had kept substantially its basic

ecclesial traditions and had developed its own heritage on lines
that can be traced back to the beginning.

II

THESE CHURCHES HAVE THEIR OWN HERITAGE

In order to promote reunion with the non-Catholic Eastern
Churches, the Catholic Church has declared several times since
the break that she would respect their individual character in
matters of discipline and liturgy as long as unity of doctrine was
safeguarded. Undoubtedly, in spite of the generous intention behind these gestures, what was granted to the Eastern Churches
was only a recognition of "privileges" within a Catholic unity that
was considered monolithic. They were exceptions and in order to
create conditions favorable to reunion, their rites and usages were
to be respected. This attitude contained an element of undeniable
generosity, particularly where the great popes were concerned who
did all they could to protect the authentic heritage of those Eastern
Christians who were in union with Rome, and this needs to be said.
Leo XIII, Benedict XV and Pius XI treated this Eastern heritage
with a nobility and loyalty which do credit to their perspicacity
which was far in advance of the attitude of contemporary Catholics. Yet, this open-mindedness brought no results. Essentially,
the East had acquired this heritage without the West, and the
recognition of privileges considered as exceptions within the unity
of Latin Catholics, whether in fact or by right, was hardly satisfactory. It could not see there the image of its own authentic
physiognomy. That is why the Decree on Ecumenism wanted to
alter the perspective and to put the traditional patrimony of the
East in direct relation with the apostolic origin of the various
Eastern Churches. In this it merely followed the line laid down in
the Constitution on the Church. The diversity of rite, culture and
spiritual heritage is directly related to an ecclesiology based on a
Communion of Sister Churches which have, each of them, built

up their own spiritual synthesis according to the charismata they have received from the Lord.

To understand this fact it is important to remember that the Christian faith has come from the East and was only embodied in the Latin culture long after it had assimilated the culture of the Aramaic Jews and the Greeks. The first great Christian literature did not appear until Tertullian, at the end of the 2nd century. The Greeks already possessed their great theologians, and the Syrians, who were so closely linked with the origins of the Gospel, had already begun to build up a spiritual synthesis that would characterize them for many centuries to come. While Rome became more and more the center of the Latin West, the great Churches of the East began to develop features that corresponded to their own mentality. This diversity did not harm the Church's unity, and both Greek and Latin ecclesiastical writers admitted that this variety enriched the appearance of the one Church. Eusebius, Socrates and Sozomenes saw that clearly, and St. Augustine, John the Deacon and Pope John I have passages that are no less significant on this point.

It is also in the East that the great theological problems arose and were solved within that universal unity. There, indeed, the basic tenets of our faith were formulated definitively. The great doctrinal crises were solved in the first seven Ecumenical Councils, which are enduring monuments of the Christian faith. These Councils of the first centuries were all held in the East. Although in most of them the papal legates played a most important part, it remains a fact that this theological confrontation showed a vitality of thought proper to the East. There never was, and even today there is not, a Christian East: there are only various Eastern Churches which contributed, each in her own way, to the enrichment of the doctrinal and spiritual heritage of the universal Church. If the East had been as monolithic as the Latin West, it would not have produced that spiritual wealth which has become the common treasure of all the Churches and on which the Latin world has continued to nourish itself for many centuries.

One of the most remarkable features of the spiritual heritage of the East, directly related to its own ecclesiology, is the connection between its conception of the Trinity and the life of the Church. As a Communion of Sister Churches it considers the Trinity first in the divine Persons and then proceeds to affirm their one nature. In contrast, the West, following Tertullian and Augustine, begins with the divine monarchy and then proceeds to consider the Trinity of the divine Persons.

At the beginning of this address I drew attention to the three relations, which appear in the inspired text itself, between the divine Persons, their unity and the communion of all in the one Body of Christ. This shows a profound aspect of theology, the importance of which Western thought has hardly begun to see as it becomes more familiar with Eastern sources. The Constitution on the Liturgy as well as the Constitution on the Church have incorporated this perspective, though timidly. It must be stressed that up till the present day this perspective has always lain at the heart of Orthodox thought. Some contemporary Orthodox theologians may have been tempted to exaggerate its importance at the expense of other no less traditional aspects of the mystery and the structure which Christ has willed for his Church. Nevertheless, it cannot be denied that in the East the mystery of the Church is not only understood but lived in close connection with the mystery of the Trinity. And it is equally certain that this theology is deeply rooted in the thought of the early Church. It is enough to refer again to St. Ignatius of Antioch.

Seeing the Church's life essentially in the light of worship and liturgy, Eastern spirituality tends in principle to make man return to the Father under the guidance of the Spirit through the mystery of Christ the Savior. That is why one can say, according to one's point of view, that the Eastern Christian is essentially "pneumatic" (centered on the Spirit), since life in the Spirit through prayer and sacraments is the essential condition for access to divine life; or that it is basically "christological" insofar as his liturgy is centered on the paschal mystery, his prayer concentrates on assimilation with Christ, and his devotion to Mary is wholly based on the

Ephesian dogma of Mary as the *Theotokos*, the Mother of God.

To sum up, both liturgy and spirituality tend to give a trinitarian imprint to the life of the faithful by which they live the divine adoption through Christ the Savior in the Spirit.

This is one of the reasons why monasticism is at the heart of the ecclesial reality in the East. If, because of the vicissitudes of history, this is no longer as flourishing as it was in the past, the fact remains that liturgy, spirituality and monasticism are closely interconnected and that in the Eastern tradition the whole mystical life is in one way or another bound up with the asceticism and contemplation of the monks.

We know, moreover, that the West received the monastic life from the East and that it is Western monastic life that has been one of the most powerful factors in maintaining an effective contact between the East and the Latin world.

All these elements have helped to build up the specific character of the Eastern Churches, and up to the present, the Orthodox have remained acutely aware of this. The Orthodox Churches, inheritors of these treasures by which they live, must therefore be certain of being taken for what they are. The Christian East cannot be considered in any sense as a kind of appendix to Western Christendom. We have to deal with Churches that are sources on which the West has constantly drawn in the past and whose true patrimony must be respected in its integrity if our wish for a dialogue is to be taken seriously.

This requires, on the part of the Catholic Church, an attitude of self-denial, of spiritual poverty, which disposes her to rediscover and assimilate the treasures of others if she wishes to be truly Catholic. And if this is true for the Church's attitude toward contemporary cultures, it is even more evident that this attitude of evangelical poverty must show itself first in standing open to Christian traditions which have become unfortunately somewhat alien to her or which the Latin world has never fully understood. This is a matter which involves the true catholicity of the Church and the possibility of finding once more the unity we lost.

III

THE EASTERN CHURCHES MUST BE KNOWN AND RESPECTED

Having admitted that the Eastern Churches have preserved the essence of their ecclesial nature and have transmitted an authentic patrimony inherited from the apostles, the decree has therefore returned to a perspective without which a genuine dialogue cannot even be started. It still had to draw the practical consequences. The first task the Council undertook was therefore to affirm solemnly the legitimacy of this specific heritage and the duty of all the faithful to get to know it and to respect it. It is specially noteworthy that in this document the Council has repeatedly used most solemn formulas to confirm the right of the Eastern Churches to live according to their own traditions. It is no longer a question of "privileges", or tolerated exceptions, as has been said already, but of rights and duties. The conciliar text says explicitly that this recognition is a preliminary condition of the dialogue. In other words, there is no hope for a reunion of East and West unless these facts are recognized explicitly and these right are sanctioned.

The Council warns us, therefore, that in order to work for reunion we have to pay special attention to the nature of the bond that united the Eastern Churches and the See of Rome from the beginning. Because of its ecclesiology based on communion between the Churches and because of the apostolic origin of its oldest Churches, the East had links with Rome of a kind which the Western Churches have never known: these Western Churches all owe their foundation more or less directly to the Church of Rome, the only definitely apostolic Church in the Western world.

The Council also recommends Catholics to go to the sources of Eastern spirituality in order to live more completely in the plenitude of the Christian tradition. But its most solemn declaration concerns the discipline that belongs specifically to the East. The unfortunate experience of certain Uniate Churches who have been absorbed by the Latin character of the West could make the

Eastern Churches fear that, once union has been established, they will be overwhelmed by the weight of the Western Church, which is more universal and better organized. In the few sentences of paragraph 16 of the decree, the Fathers of the Council, practically all Latin, have taken on an immense responsibility which will dispel those fears.

Some may regret that the text of the decree has not explicitly sanctioned the rights of the Patriarchs. Those who know how to read these documents will see that the Patriarchs are formally mentioned in the new draft of paragraph 14 where it is recognized that the patriarchal Churches occupy the first place among the local Churches several of which are of apostolic origin. Moreover, the fact that the specific heritage of the Eastern Churches is recognized as legitimate, and the obligation to maintain their own discipline integrally (contrary to what may have happened in the past in the case of certain Uniate Churches) show that this institution, so vitally important in the East, and the autocephalous character of several Churches will be respected.

There was, however, another reason apparently why the Patriarchates and their rights were not dealt with explicitly. At the end of the Bull *Laetentur Coeli*, which proclaimed the union of Greeks and Latins, the Council of Florence firmly declared that their rights and privileges would be maintained in full. One has to admit that this declaration did not tally with the practice of the Church and the contemporary state of ecclesiology. The first step should have been to take note of the actual situation, of what the Eastern Churches are and what their relations were with Rome and among themselves during the time when they were still happily in full communion with one another. Vatican II concentrated on bringing its ecclesiology up to date together with all those sectors of the Church's life that depend on this ecclesiology more or less directly. Some time will still be necessary before these carefully drafted texts can bear fruit. The liturgy, the *De Ecclesia*, and the *De Munere Episcoporum* must first prove themselves before it is possible to give serious and explicit undertakings which grant the specific nature of the Eastern Patriarchates its true and full value.

Would there not be something wrong in solemnly binding oneself to the legitimacy and obligatory maintenance of an institution that presupposes collegial power in the Church when we have only just rediscovered the true meaning of this power? Is a silence that leaves intact what the Catholic Church had subscribed to in Florence not better than precipitate declarations before there has been a chance of any practical applications? Christian prudence should be at the root of our ecumenical activity. We cannot propose more than we are actually capable of giving. We need time and must let the Spirit act. The things of God mature but slowly, and we should seriously think first of putting our own house in order before pretending to reestablish institutions of which we, Latins, have never fully understood the ecclesiological implications.

On another point, however, the Council has shown great courage. I alluded to it at the beginning of this talk and it concerns the *communicatio in sacris*. This is in many ways a very delicate problem. Latin discipline, formulated mainly since the Counter-Reformation, was very rigid on this point and gradually extended its intransigent attitude, first aimed only at the Protestant denominations of the 16th century, to all denominations that did not recognize the primacy of Rome. The dynamic influence of the ecumenical movement brought new urgency to this question of *communicatio in sacris*, or, as it is called in ecumenical language, intercommunion. Pope Paul himself broke with this too legalistic tradition in certain ecumenical gestures that did not fail to make their point. His symbolic gesture of offering a chalice to all the Eastern Patriarchs he met in Jerusalem was of great theological importance. One does not offer a chalice to leaders of a Church if one considers their eucharistic celebration unlawful. He was even more explicit in his message to the Rhodes Conference: "May love, nourished at the table of the Lord, make us every day more concerned about the unity of the Spirit in the bond of peace." Does this not underline eloquently the text of the Decree on Ecumenism where it says that in celebrating the eucharist the Orthodox Churches grow into the One Church of God?

One can understand, therefore, how the decree could lay down, not only that *communicatio in sacris* with non-Catholic Eastern Churches is possible, obviously in clearly defined circumstances, but that it is to be recommended. The general principles of this extension of *communicatio in sacris* are laid down in paragraph 8 of Chapter II, which deals with ecumenical practice for Catholics. As the text admits, it is certain that, since *communicatio in sacris* is a sign of unity, it cannot be applied where this unity does not exist. But a second principle is brought into play: there are cases where to abstain from intercommunion could be a scandal for the faithful and harden divisions that are only superficial. This is sometimes the case in the Near East. Therefore, the grace given by the sacraments or common prayer may make this *communicatio in sacris* commendable in certain cases. There is no conflict here between the Church's teaching and a practice that is opposed to it, but it is rather a matter of two facets of one and the same question, namely, that the life of grace in the Church, the communion which is lived in unity, may sometimes prevent this intercommunion and sometimes make it necessary.

One should, however, beware of an attitude that is oversimplified. *Communicatio in sacris* touches the very heart of the mystery of the Church's unity and can therefore not be treated lightheartedly. Still less should it be used as a means of immature proselytism. It presupposes as a *conditio sine quo non* that both parties agree to it consciously and loyally, so that no harm is done to the work of ecumenism. In no case must it be a matter of isolated individuals. It necessarily involves the leaders of the two Churches in question. To be a step toward full communion between us and our Eastern brothers, Catholic and Orthodox bishops must explicitly agree to it. These latter have qualities that essentially belong to the true Church, and this is admitted. We may, therefore, suggest intercommunion to them, but we can in no way impose it nor practice it without their knowledge. This would go completely against the spirit that the decree wishes to inculcate: to respect these non-Catholic Churches as Churches. To practice intercommunion without their knowledge or consent would imply a denial of their ecclesial character.

On the contrary, it is precisely our recognition of the ecclesial character of these Churches that makes it possible for us to propose this intercommunion to them as a means of grace by which we can come closer together in view of full and final union. In the past, Churchmen were wrong in this matter of reunion with the East. They laid down conditions which were the object of diplomatic negotiations, which, it was hoped, would lead to an agreement to restore intercommunion. But when one has realized that theologically the marks of the true Church are sufficiently, though from our point of view incompletely, present among our brothers of the East, one is entitled to suggest intercommunion if the circumstances are opportune. With the help of God's grace in us we can then try to find the formula that will make full and unconditional intercommunion possible.

All these points are extremely important to start the dialogue with the East. It must not remain a monologue, but should be a true exchange of genuine values. With us, ecumenism has entered upon a new phase, and henceforth our attitude toward the Eastern Churches will no longer be the same, if the decree is taken as seriously as it deserves. Nothing has changed in the basic teaching of our faith. On the contrary, what has happened is that we have become more fully aware of the rich and complex reality of the Church's heritage. This will lead us to that one true catholicity that accepts all genuine Christian traditions in their totality to the glory of the Father, Son and Holy Spirit in the One Holy Church of God.

PART IV

CHRONICLE OF THE
LIVING CHURCH

IN COLLABORATION WITH
KATHOLIEK ARCHIEF
Amersfoort, Netherlands

Edward Schillebeeckx, O.P./*Nijmegen, Netherlands*

The Tridentine Decree on Justification: A New View

Professor Heiko A. Oberman, well-known for his great work, *The Harvest of Mediaeval Theology. G. Biel and Late Mediaeval Nominalism* (Cambridge, Mass., 1963), recently published an important article on the Tridentine justification decree in the light of late mediaeval theology ("Das tridentinische Rechtfertigungsdekret im Lichte spätmittelalterlicher Theologie," in *Zeitschrift für Theologie und Kirche* 61 (1964), pp. 251–82). His main conclusions are as follows: when the Council of Trent condemned the thesis that man by himself can merit his justification, it only wished to exclude explicitly the *merita de condigno*, merits in the strict sense of the word (as a due). It purposely used the term *promereri* as opposed to *mereri* (referring to the *meritum de congruo:* not meriting in the strict sense).

The assertion that man can merit grace by his own strength but not as if it were a due, was not condemned by the Council. Therefore, says Oberman, Trent needs to be corrected because the Council left open the question of the *meritum de congruo*. This concept offends the Reformed view, and the protest of the Reformation remains valid.

It seems to me that the analysis of the texts in themselves and in the light of late mediaeval theology made by Professor Oberman, a Reformed Christian himself, is unanswerable and historically correct. Indeed, Franciscan Scotists and nominalistic theologians

176

of that period maintained that man cannot strictly merit the "first grace" (*prima gratia*), but that God in his abundant love will not refuse his grace to whoever tries to do his best with his *own* human strength. They called this *mereri* or the *meritum de congruo* as opposed to *promereri* or the *meritum de condigno*. This offended the Reformers the more as it underrated the absolute and sovereign gratuitousness of grace.

The Dominican Thomists agreed with the Reformers: they denied any predisposition which was not first given as a grace, in whatever form. They saw in man's *self*-sufficiency, as *opposed* to grace, a form of Pelagianism. Apart from the now outdated concepts and formulation in which these Thomists expressed themselves, we may say that their concept of grace is today commonly accepted as part of Roman Catholic spirituality, although here and there the old ideas persist. Contemporary Catholic theology, which emphasizes the omnipresent activity of "anonymous grace" and affirms that all free human activity stands under the grace of God, has already for some time broken with any semi-Pelagian tendencies.

While I accept Oberman's analysis of the Tridentine texts, I would like to add one or two precisions to his evaluation of them (and I think these would fall in line with his own underlying intentions). One cannot really say that the dogma of Trent decided *in favor* of the Scotist and nominalistic *meritum de congruo*, by which man can prepare himself for God's grace and so merit it by his own strength on the basis of God's liberality, not God's justice. In spite of the pressures that were brought to bear, Trent maintained its principle of not defining anything on which the three parties, Thomists, Scotists and nominalists, were not agreed. In this sense the Tridentine definition limits itself to the minimum, an action that was and still is repugnant to the Reformers, and rightly so.

What Trent needs urgently from the ecumenical point of view is not a correction (Oberman uses the word "Korrektur", p. 282) but an addition, because in the decree of Trent the Church leaves open the *possibility* that man can prepare himself for grace in some way and not in the strict sense by his own strength and without grace. Dominican Thomism has always felt ill at ease with some Tridentine texts, or tried, without historical justification, to "pull" Trent in its own direction.

For some time I had been worrried about the unsatisfactory features of some texts of Trent, and Oberman has brought them out more clearly. This dogma is not the *complete answer* which the Reformers may ask of Catholic spirituality and theology. Trent's answer is not incorrect, but incomplete. The Catholic Church has more to say about the absolute priority of grace than she has expressed in the dogma of Trent. And this dogma must also be interpreted in the light of late mediaeval theological controversy.

Ecumenically speaking, we would like to see Vatican II not only supplement Vatican I but also the Council of Trent. What Trent said in the language of its own period is a positive part of the Catholic faith, but more needs saying. Only then can all kinds of misunderstandings be eliminated and can we see more clearly how the Reformed concept of "borrowing" or "lending" differs from the Catholic one of "meriting".

Here we should take seriously into account what Reinhard Kösters wrote recently in his article on Luther's thesis of "just and sinner at the same time" ("Luther's These: Gerecht und Sünder zugleich," in *Catholica* 18 [1964], pp. 193–217), namely, that the teaching on justification is legal only and does not imply a denial of the true renewal of man. Before him C. Berkouwer had already pointed out ("Verdienste of genade?", Kampen, 1958, p. 61) that the expressions, "legal", "imputative" and "declaratory" are by no means identical with "external"; the Reformation was mainly concerned with the aspect of "from above", of grace as truly supreme, and this, too, is part of Catholic faith.

It must, however, be remembered in this controversy that the Catholic expression *sola gratia* does not imply that God alone operates. Every grace of God is strictly *divine*, *i.e.*, it creates out of nothing and gratuitously. But precisely because every grace is creative, man himself becomes indeed the *active* subject of grace.

And so grace itself becomes a visible, tangible, *historical* reality *in* man's freedom. If an older terminology treated these realities perhaps too much as if they were "things", this is but a side aspect due to an historical condition. The deeper meaning was that the aspect of grace as an "incarnation", an historical reality, was essential to Christianity.

This has been made clear insofar as St. Thomas is concerned in a recent study by M. Seckler on historical theology in Thomas Aquinas (*Das Heil in der Geschichte. Geschichtstheologisches Denken bei Thomas von Aquin*, Munich, 1964). A. Hulsbosch pointed to the same aspect in an article on hermeneutics ("Het hermeneutische beginsel," in *Tijdschrift voor Theologie* 5 [1965]) where he compared Catholicism with the theories of R. Bultmann; he calls the inability to see the historicity and incarnation of grace in human and earthly form "the blind spot" of the Reformation.

The core of the controversy, "merit *or* grace?" then falls in a very different perspective, where Christology and Pneumatology can neither be separated nor opposed, so that we can say with 1 John 1, 1: We have touched the Mystery with our own hands. What our human freedom contains in manifestation and "translation" of God's grace cannot be considered to be in competition with God's grace in itself. That is why merit and grace are never opposed to each other: within the *telos* or end, given us as a pledge or *arrha* by the indwelling Spirit, we are borne toward the future *in* our historical existence.

There is, therefore, an inner proportion between the life of grace on this earth and life in the everlasting kingdom. This proportion rests on that very grace that realizes the human answer to grace, and it is this that makes the Catholic Church speak of "merit". The word is not important, but the content *is:* merit indicates the historicity of the supremacy of grace within human freedom, and in no sense competes with *sola gratia*.

Franz Böckle / *Bonn, W. Germany*

Foundation of the
Societas Ethica *not for Refectory*

Exegetes of the principal Christian denominations have already collaborated usefully for years. They organized themselves into the *Societas Neo-Testamentica* and meet at an annual congress to their mutual advantage. For some time a few individuals connected with the publication of the *Zeitschrift für evangelische Ethik* (Gütersloher Verlagshaus, Gerd Mohn) have tried to organize something similar for those teaching Christian ethics.

An impressive number of university teachers met in Basle (October 9–11, 1964) in order to found a *Societas ethica*. They were mainly drawn from evangelical-reformed faculties, and came from Helsinki, Oslo, Lund, Copenhagen, Amsterdam, Strasbourg, Debrecen, Bratislava and from all over Germany. Unfortunately, there were only a few representatives from Catholic theological faculties. The participants did not want to limit themselves exclusively to a discussion of articles of association and programs, but immediately plunged into a discussion of an actual topic: "The Theological Foundation of Ethics in View of the Modern Demand for a 'New Morality' ". The introductory papers were read by Professor Mehl of Strasbourg for the Evangelical side and Professor W. Schöllgen of Bonn for the Catholic side.

The most stimulating discussion hinged around the question whether further work should start with the problem of principles or with concrete and actual topics (*e.g.*, marriage) and then continue by the inductive method. After this discussion the society was set up officially. Professor F. Böckle was asked to represent the Catholics on the Committee.

The first annual congress will be held this year, from August 30 to September 2 in Basle. The subject will be "Marriage from the Point of View of Sociology, Exegesis and Ethics". The present president of the society is Professor Dr. H. van Oyen, Basle; and the secretarial management has been put into the hands of Dr. K. Bockmühl, CH-4153-Reinach, Lachenweg 36, Switzerland.

BIOGRAPHICAL NOTES

COENRAAD A.J. VAN OUWERKERK, C.SS.R.: Born July 15, 1923 in Hilversum, Netherlands. He became a Redemptorist, and was ordained in 1948. He studied at the Angelicum and at the Academia Alfonsiana in Rome, and at the Catholic University of Nijmegen, Netherlands, earning his doctorate in theology in 1956. He is Professor of Moral Theology and Pastoral Psychology at the Redemptorist House in Wittem, Netherlands, and is a member of the Pastoral Commission of the Katholieke Vereniging van Geestleijke Volksgezondheid.

JAN HENRICUS WALGRAVE, O.P.: Born April 30, 1911. He became a Dominican, and was ordained in 1935. He studied at the University of Louvain where he earned his doctorate in theology. He has published several works, and is an active contributor to *Kultuurleven* and *Tijdschrift voor Theologie*.

JOSEPH T.C. ARNTZ, O.P.: Born May 20, 1919 in Nijmegen, Netherlands. He became a Dominican, and was ordained in 1943. He studied at the Catholic University of Nijmegen, Netherlands, where he earned his doctorates in theology, philosophy and letters. He is Professor of Ethics at the Dominican House of Studies in Zwolle, Netherlands. He has published a number of books, and contributes articles regularly to the *Irish Theological Quarterly*.

GERHARD JOHANNES BOTTERWECK: Born April 25, 1917 in Rheydt, Germany, he was ordained in 1944. He studied at the Universities of Frankfurt-Main, Vienna and Bonn. He earned his doctorate in Oriental Philology and Archaeology at University of Vienna in 1944, and his doctorate in theology at the University of Bonn in 1950. From 1953 to 1959 he was Professor of Old Testament Theology at the University of Tübingen. Since 1959 he has been Professor of Old Testament Studies at the University of Bonn. In addition to several published works, he has contributed numerous articles on exegesis and Old Testament theology to various periodicals.

RENÉ COSTE: Born September 29, 1922 in Saint-Genest-Lerpt, France, he was ordained in 1946. He pursued his studies at the Institut Catholique of Paris and of Toulouse, and in the Faculty of Law of the University of Toulouse, where he earned doctorates in civil and canon law in 1961. At one time Professor of Sacred Scripture at the Seminaire de la Mission de France, he is at present Professor of Canon Law at the University of Toulouse, a Director of the University Seminary of Pius XI (Toulouse) and a member of the Doctrinal Commission of the French branch of *Pax Christi* in Paris. His published works deal primarily with the morality of war, and he is a regular contributor to various journals.

FRANZ BÖCKLE: Born April 18, 1921, in Glarus, Switzerland, he was ordained in 1945 for the diocese of Coire. He studied at the Angelicum in Rome and at the University of Munich, earning his doctorate in theology in 1952. He has been Professor of Moral Theology at the seminary in Chur, Switzerland,

and is at present Professor at the University of Bonn. His published works deal with general ethical and moral problems (the ethics of the Evangelical Church, natural law and similar subjects).

ENDA McDONAGH: Born June 27, 1930 in County Mayo, Ireland, he was ordained in 1955. He studied at St. Patrick's College, Maynooth, the Angelicum and Gregorianum in Rome, and at the Ludwig-Maximilian University in Munich. He earned his doctorate in theology in 1957 and his doctorate in canon law in 1960. At present he is Professor of Moral Theology and Canon Law at Maynooth, Ireland, and summer lecturer in moral theology at the Catholic University of America in Washington, D.C. His published works include *Roman Catholics and Unity* (London, 1962). He is editor of the symposium, *The Meaning of Christian Marriage* (Dublin, 1963), and is a regular contributor to such periodicals as the *Irish Theological Quarterly* and *The Furrow*.

GIACOMO CARDINAL LERCARO: Born October 27, 1891 in Quinto al Mare, Italy, he was ordained in 1914. Among several institutions of higher learning, he studied at the Biblicum in Rome, and holds a doctorate in theology. He is Professor of Sacred Scripture and Patristics at Genoa, President of the Commission for the Implementation of the Constitution on the Sacred Liturgy, and Vice-President of Italy's Apostolate for the Liturgy. He is Archbishop of Bologna, Italy.

EDWARD SCHILLEBEECKX, O.P.: Born November 12, 1914 in Antwerp, Belgium. He became a Dominican in 1934, and was ordained in 1941. He pursued his studies at Le Saulchoir and at the Sorbonne, becoming a master and doctor of theology. From 1943 to 1957 he taught at the Dominican House of Studies in Louvain, Belgium, and has been, since 1958, Professor of Dogmatic Theology at the University of Nijmegen, Netherlands. He is an advisor to the Dutch episcopacy at Vatican Council II. Among his many published works are: *The Sacramental Economy of Salvation* (1952); *Christ, the Sacrament of the Encounter with God* (1963); *Mary, Mother of the Redemption* (1964); *Huwelijk, aardse werkelijkheid en heilsmysterie,* Vol. I (1964).